TWIN CITIES

TWIN CITIES

MY LIFE AS A BLACK COP AND
A CHAMPIONSHIP COACH

CHARLES ADAMS

WITH JASON TURBOW

hachette
BOOKS
New York

Hachette Books
Hachette Book Group
1290 Avenue of the Americas
New York, NY 10104
HachetteBooks.com
Twitter.com/HachetteBooks
Instagram.com/HachetteBooks

First Edition: September 2023

Published by Hachette Books, an imprint of Hachette Book Group, Inc.
The Hachette Books name and logo is a trademark of the Hachette Book Group.

The Hachette Speakers Bureau provides a wide range of authors for speaking events. To find out more, go to hachettespeakersbureau.com or email HachetteSpeakers@hbgusa.com.

Books by Hachette Books may be purchased in bulk for business, educational, or promotional use. For information, please contact your local bookseller or Hachette Book Group Special Markets Department at special.markets@hbgusa.com.

The publisher is not responsible for websites (or their content) that are not owned by the publisher.

Print book interior design by Bart Dawson.

Library of Congress Cataloging-in-Publication Data
Names: Adams, Charles (Police), author. | Turbow, Jason, author.
Title: Twin cities : my life as a Black cop and a championship coach / Charles Adams with Jason Turbow.
Description: First edition. | New York, NY : Hachette Books, 2023.
Identifiers: LCCN 2023017577 | ISBN 9780306830549 (hardcover) | ISBN 9780306830563 (ebook)
Subjects: LCSH: Adams, Charles (Police) | Police—Minnesota—Minneapolis—Biography. | Police, Black—Minnesota—Minneapolis—Biography. | School police—Minnesota—Minneapolis—Biography. | Football coaches—Minnesota—Minneapolis—Biography. | Minneapolis (Minn.)—Race relations. | Racism in law enforcement—Minnesota—Minneapolis. | Black lives matter movement—Minnesota—Minneapolis.
Classification: LCC HV7911.A258 A3 2023 | DDC 363.2092 [B]—dc23/eng/20230503
LC record available at https://lccn.loc.gov/2023017577

ISBNs: 978-0-306-83054-9 (hardcover), 978-0-306-83056-3 (ebook)

Printed in the United States of America

LSC-C

Printing 1, 2023

To my loving wife and kids,
Andreaua, Adrian, Anya, Anyla, and Audria.
You are my source of inspiration and support.

CONTENTS

Dear Lord, the battles we go through life
We ask for a chance that's fair
A chance to equal our stride,
A chance to do or dare

If we should win, let it be by the code,
Faith and honor held high
If we should lose, we'll stand by the road,
And cheer as the winners go by

Day by day, we get better and better
Til' we can't be beat . . .
Won't be beat!

—"Husker Prayer," adapted from
"Prayer of a Sportsman" by Berton Braley

TWIN CITIES

INTRODUCTION

Another Black man got shot by another cop, the latest in a long string of incidents here in Minneapolis and beyond. Police had burst into an apartment using a no-knock warrant and found Amir Locke asleep on a couch, wrapped in a blanket. Amir had a gun with him, legal and licensed, and though he never aimed it at anyone—he'd only just been startled awake— within nine seconds of entry the police had shot him dead. Amir's name wasn't even on the warrant; he'd spent the night at his cousin's place and found himself the focus of some tragic circumstances.

That happened early in 2022, two years and three and a half miles from where George Floyd had been killed by police. Minneapolis residents were desperate to end these slayings.

I am the head football coach at North Community High School in Minneapolis, the city's poorest school in the city's poorest neighborhood. For twenty years I was also a member of the Minneapolis Police Department. The last two of those years covered the Floyd incident and its aftermath. It was a hell of a combination, but I made it work because the kids knew me, I knew them, and everybody respected each other.

At North High, 90 percent of the student body is Black, so it shouldn't be difficult to guess how most of our kids felt about this police violence. To her credit, our school's principal, Mauri Friestleben, saw the Amir Locke situation as a learning opportunity and in the wake of protests across the city encouraged our students to execute a walkout of their own. She even joined them in a sit-in at city hall. The merits of those decisions can be debated forever, but what came next could not have been foreseen by anyone.

At lunchtime on February 9, 2022, while a mass of protesting North High kids left campus for a rally downtown, one of them decided to go home instead. That was Deshaun Hill's plan, anyway. While walking to the bus stop, he found himself in the wrong place at the wrong time, brushing shoulders with a stranger on the sidewalk. Deshaun didn't seem to think much of it; security camera footage shows him not even breaking stride. The other guy, though, turned, pulled out a gun, and squeezed off three shots. Deshaun did not survive the encounter.

Deshaun was an extraordinary kid, an honor-roll student, and my starting quarterback. We called him D-Hill. He was only a sophomore. His is not some stereotypical inner-city tragedy of a teenager caught up in a life on the streets. It is the story of a young man poised to rise above . . . and a reminder that, despite our best efforts, our neighborhood's challenges are sometimes inescapable. As Deshaun's family wrote in the aftermath of his killing, he was "a representation of what could be, what should be."

Gun violence is commonplace in my neighborhood, the Northside of Minneapolis. More people are shot there than anywhere in the state. You might think that would make it the toughest part of town to be a cop, but for me it was home. That's where I grew up, attending North High, just like both of my parents. I have spent my entire adult life looking out for the well-being of my neighborhood, which for thirteen years included working as the school resource officer at my alma mater, an on-campus policeman serving as a conduit between our community and the Minneapolis Police Department. I can't think of a better beat.

Hometown pride means different things to different people, but on the Northside, home to so much violence and commotion, outspoken proponents for our neighborhood are vital. I will never stop being an advocate, yet my working for an employer known for killing Black people became a massive issue. After George Floyd's murder, it's remarkable how a lifetime spent walking the walk seemed to matter so little. In June 2020, within a week of the first protests, the school board terminated its contract with the MPD, canceling my position on campus and putting me back onto the street in a patrol car. So much of the goodwill I'd exactingly built over decades was wiped away almost overnight, simply because of the uniform I continued to wear.

None of that changed my devotion to the neighborhood or the school. Even though I could no longer serve as North High's resource officer, I stayed on as the school's football coach—and will continue to do so for as long as they'll have me.

My job is why I was among the first people called when news about Deshaun Hill began to circulate. The first person I heard from was my friend Marcus, a security monitor at the school. He'd just seen something about an incident posted on social media. "Do you know what's going on with D-Hill?" he asked. "People are saying he got shot on Golden Valley Road and Penn Avenue. You better call your dad and find out what's going on."

My father, Charles Adams II, is a big piece of the puzzle that has been my career. As of this writing he's been a Minneapolis cop for thirty-five years, rising through the ranks to become the inspector in charge of the entire Fourth Precinct, where North High is located. I called, but he was in a meeting and did not pick up. Now I was growing frantic. My phone rang again. It was Lamar, another member of North High's support staff. "Nobody knows anything for sure, but there are videos on Facebook," he said. "I can't say for sure it's D-Hill, but I see a blue backpack that looks like his, and somebody lying on the ground with a boot." Shit. D-Hill was wearing a walking boot after a recent football injury. I got a text from Tom Lachermeier, a history teacher at North and one of my assistants on the football team: "Please, please tell me I'm not hearing what I think I'm hearing."

By that point we were all hearing it.

In addition to being a high-ranking cop, my father is one of my assistant coaches at North High and knew Deshaun well.

Dad told me later that he'd had grave doubts about the student walkout—not with the protest per se, but with where it would occur. Kids from wealthier parts of Minneapolis could walk out all day long, he said, but our neighborhood is dangerous enough just getting to and from school. Leaving campus in the middle of the day without organized security seemed like too much. Dad thought about calling Mauri, our principal, with his concern, but as is the case with many ideas, life got in the way and he never picked up the phone. It haunts him to this day. Then again, a detail protecting the protestors would have done nothing for Deshaun. Sometimes there are no good answers.

Dad had just emerged from that meeting in his Fourth Precinct office when he got word of a fifteen-year-old male being shot. He immediately dialed school administrators, one after the other, without success. By the time Mauri called back, he'd just received the devastating confirmation that it was indeed Deshaun on that sidewalk, and that the outlook was grim. They both broke down completely, two messes of tears on the telephone. Dad's sadness was uncontrollable, and I knew exactly how he felt. It was sorrow, and also confusion. That kind of thing happening to any of my players would break me up, but I know better than anyone the kinds of dangerous situations some of those guys put themselves into. It'd be ignorant to think that my team is immune to the dangerous lifestyle choices made by so many people in our neighborhood. D-Hill, though? He was clean, with a bright future ahead of him. None of it made sense.

I told Lachermeier to get the football players down to the weight room, and that I'd be there within thirty minutes. As I drove, my mind raced. Why had Deshaun been neither on campus nor at the protest? Why did he go in the opposite direction of his classmates? Why couldn't he have stayed put? Cops make up a significant portion of my coaching staff, and although we never deterred the players from expressing their beliefs, I knew that many of them would avoid protesting against the police. Still, I couldn't help thinking that if D-Hill had just joined in, had walked downtown with the rest of them, he'd still be fine. We all would.

I was about five minutes away from school when a friend from the force called. The police had thoroughly reviewed the video and confirmed everything I'd heard. "He was all but dead when we got there, man," the officer told me. He said that Deshaun was on life support at the hospital, less out of hope for survival than to give family members a chance to say goodbye. I was crushed, yet the statement sparked the faintest hope that D-Hill still had a chance. He was alive, and that was something.

That was my final thought before I pulled into the school's parking lot. The kids were gathered in the weight room, along with the coaches and even some parents. Grief counselors had already been called. As a police officer, I've been on the scene of dozens of homicides, and I have spoken to countless relatives of victims. Nothing I'd done with the department came close to this. I had to address my team at a moment when there were no words, so I told them what I would be doing for the next several hours: praying for D-Hill. I urged them to do the same. If he was alive, no matter how long the chances, faith was all we had left.

It wasn't enough. Deshaun died not long thereafter.

Over the coming days we opened up space on campus for students to talk. The football team spent the next week together with no expectations, only opportunities for kids to express themselves. We're here with you, we're here for you, even as we are deep in mourning ourselves. Our weight room turned into a therapy center, at first with professionals and then with coaches, especially Lachermeier, making space for players to share whatever seemed right in the moment. A lot of kids, especially young African American men, are reluctant to open up and share their feelings. We tried to normalize it for them at least a little bit. I think it helped.

After D-Hill's shooting, the Minneapolis *Star Tribune* wrote that the incident "has led to renewed calls for a more forceful response to violence that has afflicted the city's Northside for generations." Well, no shit. I've been hearing that line since I attended North High back in the 1990s. Deshaun isn't even the first player I've lost. Nate Hampton, who played for me for two years before transferring to Thomas Edison High School in 2015, and Charles Royston, a starting cornerback on our 2016 championship team, both fell to gun violence after they'd graduated. Just this last March, one of my players, Cashmere "Cash" Grunau—a junior who'd been teammates with D-Hill—was shot while walking near his house, about ten blocks from North High. Thankfully, he was hit only in his legs and is expected to fully recover. It's devastating, all of it, but that seems to be the way things go in our neighborhood. In 2019, North High student Keimonte White was gunned down. In 2020 another

North High student, Diontae Wallace, was shot and killed. The same day Deshaun was murdered in 2022, only blocks away, a school bus driver—with three young children on board—was shot in the head. The day after that, less than a mile from the high school, two men were shot and killed inside a car. Looking in from the outside, it can be difficult to see beyond the violence. That's the only impression most people have of our hood. They think that every kid is on welfare or that their families are full of gangbangers, and that's just not true. I know, because I work there. I know, because I coach the kids at the other end of those presumptions. More than that, I *am* one of those kids. So are my dad, my mom, my uncle—we're all from the Northside. We all went to North High. Well, it *is* the hood, and it *is* rough. Shit, my quarterback was killed walking to the fucking bus stop. But there is so much good in our community, and that's what I'm trying to bring out.

My dad put his former partner from the homicide department, Lt. Richard Zimmerman—one of the city's best detectives—on the Hill case, and a suspect was quickly brought into custody. He was twenty-nine years old, with a significant criminal history and zero ties to Deshaun Hill. My guy was simply unlucky, in the worst possible way.

My whole team sat together at the funeral. I don't think I realized until that moment how lost I actually was. Being together reinforced the connection among us as a team, and between our team and the community around us. That gave me strength.

On March 13, 2022, what would have been D-Hill's sixteenth birthday, Minnesota governor Tim Walz declared Deshaun Hill Jr. Day across the state. When the 2022 football season kicked off, the North High Polars took the field one man short—no quarterback—and accepted a penalty on the first play. We did the same thing again in our next game, and every game after that, always starting with an empty space among our ranks. (After that first week, once teams understood what we were doing, they all declined the penalty.) The idea came from the players, and I was happy for it—whatever it took to help them memorialize D-Hill. Our players carried his number 9 jersey on our traditional game-day walk through the neighborhood, from school to the football field, four blocks away. We affixed a decal bearing his name and picture to every helmet, and plan to commemorate his number going forward, maybe by retiring it, or allowing one deserving player to wear it each week.

Those efforts are only tokens, but they are something, a small way to remember, and to consider the neighborhood that is so inherently part of us, for good and for bad. It's where I come from and who I am. Part of that heritage is the contradiction of constantly trying to move beyond the limits of our hometown, even as I embrace the place fully, of trying to prop it up even as I acknowledge its abundant flaws.

Coming from where I do while making the choices I've made can be complex and maddening one minute and full of inspiring beauty the next.

It's all part of being a Northsider.

·MINNEAPOLIS·

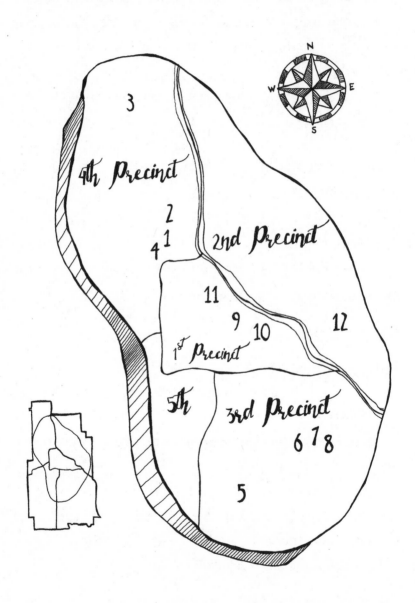

1 NORTH HIGH SCHOOL
2 22ND AVE N (FIRST HOUSE)
3 SHERIDAN AVE N (SECOND HOUSE)
4 4TH PRECINCT HEADQUARTERS
5 GEORGE FLOYD SQUARE
6 HI-LAKE SHOPPING CENTER
7 3RD PRECINCT HEADQUARTERS
8 PAWN SHOP
9 CITY HALL
10 US BANK STADIUM
11 TARGET FIELD
12 UNIVERSITY OF MINNESOTA

Chapter 1

_____

Northsider

My line to police work started with a stolen car and a misplaced accusation.

This particular story belongs to my dad, Charles Adams II, who was in the eleventh grade at North High School at the time, living in the Sumner Field housing projects on Eighth and Emerson. Dad didn't love the mice and cockroaches that scurried through his mother's apartment, or the drug deals and dice games taking place in the courtyards, but the people in those projects were like family. They looked out for the neighborhood kids and worked together to keep them in line. Dad recalls friends' grandmothers taking a switch to him when he occasionally misbehaved. People frequented each other's apartments, borrowing an egg here or a cup of sugar there. Kids went down to Johnny's Market for penny candy. Dad credits that life with providing perspective and a solid work ethic, even if his early focus was aimed primarily at escaping those projects.

Living at Sumner Field jump-started Dad's interactions with the law at an early age. He didn't like cops, which was maybe the result of cops not liking him. When Dad was in junior high, his father—my grandfather, Charles Adams—built him a minibike. Grandpa worked as a body repairman at Anderson Cadillac in southwest Minneapolis and knew his way around a motor. That bike, one of several driven by project kids, wasn't exactly legal, and whenever the police spotted one, they'd confiscate it. Should a cruiser show up while Dad and his friends were roaring through the neighborhood, they'd haul ass into the heart of the projects, down ramps too narrow for cars. Neighbors, hearing sirens and the roar of minibike engines, opened their front doors, and the boys would drive straight into the closest living room. Every door would be closed before the police rounded the corner. Dad never got caught.

That was small stuff. The incident that permanently shaped Dad's relationship with the police involved his brother Rodney, a year older, who at the time of this story was getting ready for his high school's senior prom. Rodney, like my dad, was a North High Polar, and prom at North High was a big deal. Everybody was in on it. Rodney had his tuxedo rented and was looking sharp. He also had a special ride lined up for him and his date.

Grandpa Charles was a downright artist when it came to auto body work. His side hustle was buying up wrecked cars, repairing them, and selling them in the *AutoTrader* magazine. He made a point of always keeping a couple around the house to drive himself, which meant that, come prom time, Rodney had access to the best ride in school—a gold 1977 Sedan

DeVille with a chrome grille, a naked lady hood ornament, and a big spare hanging off the trunk. That car was so beautiful my grandpa never sold it. He still has it today.

Well, Rodney picked up the car from his dad's place (his parents, my grandpa and grandma, were long since separated) and parked it on the street while he got ready for his big night. In Sumner Field, however, a gleaming Caddy tended to stick out, especially to patrolling policemen. Next thing Rodney knew, those cops were hooking the car to a tow truck. He and my father saw it through the window, and raced to the curb, shouting, "That's our dad's car!" The police had run the plates and got a mismatched hit—the plate number didn't match the registration. It'd have been even more maddening if they weren't right, but somehow the DMV had issued the wrong license plates when Grandpa salvaged the car from the junkyard several years earlier. None of us had any idea until that moment. Even then, though, you have to wonder why they bothered running the plates in the first place. The answer is easy: they didn't think a vehicle like that belonged in projects like those.

All Rodney wanted was to go to the prom. As he and my dad got into it with the cops, neighbors emerged from the surrounding houses. Everybody knew that was my grandfather's car, and watching it get towed away drove them wild. The yelling got pretty intense, until my grandmother came out and told her boys to knock it off. "Just let them take it," she said. "We'll get it back later." Rodney had to pick up his date in my grandma's car, which worked fine but was sure as hell no Sedan DeVille. The cops were so standoffish that they never even explained to

Rodney why they towed the car. Grandpa learned about the plate mix-up at the impound lot.

That incident led to The Talk that every Black parent in this country has with their kids. It's not a matter of if, but when. My grandmother sat her boys down not long thereafter and said, "Why in the world would you argue with policemen when they can pull out their guns and shoot you, and get away with it?" It's a question with no good answer.

The part that stuck with Dad most was what she said next: "If you want to solve the problem with the police, you should become a cop."

Which is exactly what he did. After a detour or two, including a job driving a bus for Metro Transit, Dad joined the force in 1986, at age twenty-two, patrolling South Minneapolis as a member of the Fifth Precinct.

That move was positive for everybody in the family, except one. Dad's father was so angry about it that he didn't speak to his son for six months, which included skipping his swearing-in ceremony. Grandpa could be like that sometimes. It wasn't that he was anti-police . . . although he might have been anti-police. Back in Arkansas, my grandmother's cousin had been arrested on suspicion of raping a white woman, even though everybody in the family knew it was a consensual affair. It was only upon being discovered that the woman cried rape rather than own up to loving a Black man. Folks down there say the sheriff was worse than Bull Connor, the notorious segregationist. The cousin was convicted, and while he was in prison got castrated. My whole family knew that story, and seeds of mistrust built from there.

That was three states and a generation away from Minnesota. When it came to Dad's decision to join the MPD, Grandpa was probably more upset that the move lopped more than a third off Dad's $30,000 bus driver salary. The police department, however, offered an array of opportunities for promotion that simply did not exist in Metro Transit.

It was the right call. Thirty years later, Dad had risen through the ranks from sergeant to lieutenant to commander to inspector in charge of the Fourth Precinct. That's the Northside, where he and I both grew up. Just as impactful, Dad's brother Tony, and two of his kids, me and my sister Brittney, followed him onto the force. We are a police family, through and through.

You know how some people say they were born into a certain type of life? Well, I was born into Minneapolis North Community High School, almost literally. My parents were teenagers when I was conceived, my dad a cornerback on the football team, my mom a cheerleader. Mom took me to North High's day care center when I was an infant so she could continue to attend class. My uncles Rodney and Tony were also Polars. Yeah, North High is in my blood. I am ingrained in it, and it is ingrained in me.

Because mom was an unmarried minor when I came around, the last name on my birth certificate is hers: Brunner. I always went by Adams, though, which my folks had legally changed when I was twelve. That's just the beginning of my family's name game. My dad is Charles Franklin Adams II, even though his dad's name is Charles Junior Adams. Grandpa's name is Junior, although he himself is not—his father was Johnny Adams. It's even more complicated than that. Dad's father was also named Charles, but Dad was actually named after my great-aunt Patsy's boyfriend, Charles Champion. They were real country down in Arkansas when it came to naming babies. Heck, my uncle Tony's middle name is Anthony. None of it makes any sense.

My mom, Djuana Brunner, had a different last name than her mom, my grandma Shirley Banks, who started off as a Brunner, changed her name when she got married and then kept it that way after she and her husband split up. Mom moved out of Grandma Shirley's house and into her brother Freddy's place not long after I was born because Grandma Shirley had just had a baby herself. That's right: my uncle, Aaron Banks, is twenty-eight days older than me. Like I said, it's complicated. To this day I don't know how Mom managed to live on the Southside and go to North High, but that's how it was. I'm thankful for it, because that's where she met my father.

Dad is a year older than Mom. He had already graduated when I was born, and was across town at Golden Valley Lutheran College, playing football and attending school on a Pell Grant. Those early days couldn't have been easy for him. In addition to carrying a full academic load plus football responsibilities, he worked the dinnertime shift as a janitor at the airport, scrubbing toilets and mopping floors to pay for my care. He took fatherhood seriously, his days starting with picking Mom and me up early at Uncle Freddy's place for a trip to North High, then heading to his own college classes. After football practice came his job at the airport, with family time slotted into whatever free moments he could find. For two years I spent weekends with Dad in his dorm room, settling into life as his little buddy.

I split a lot of my weekday time with Grandma Shirley and my *other* Grandma Shirley—Dad's mother, Shirley Adams, who I called Gramps. Once Dad graduated from college, we moved into Grandma Adams's house on the Northside of Minneapolis. Dad's brother Tony, still in high school, lived there, too. We were only about twenty minutes from Uncle Freddy's place, where Mom and I had been staying, with one vital difference: it put me in line to go to North High School.

When I was little, Grandma Banks started calling me Spanky after a character from her favorite show, *The Little Rascals*. It stuck. Today, everybody in my family calls me Spanky. I'm Uncle Spank to my nieces and nephews.

I spent virtually every summer of my childhood in El Dorado, Arkansas, where my dad's parents were from. El Dorado is about half-Black, with a poverty rate over 30 percent. Jobs were hard to come by, so someplace along the line, Grandpa Charles—we called him Pawpaw—traveled to visit family in places like Des Moines and Detroit, looking to pick up work. Eventually he landed with my great-aunt Stella in North Minneapolis and got a job at Anderson Cadillac, first washing cars, then fixing them. Before long he sent for his wife and kids. My dad was their first child conceived in Minnesota (even though he was born in El Dorado). Like me, he spent every summer until he was about seventeen down in Arkansas.

Each June I'd drive with my granddaddy some fifteen hours directly south in his gold '77 L-Dog—the same Cadillac Sedan DeVille that got towed before Uncle Rodney's prom. He dropped me off in El Dorado with my great-uncle Ronny and great-aunt Patsy, where I stayed until school started back up. I loved it down there, hanging out all summer with my cousins. I was a regular part of that family.

El Dorado was a super-small town, and I was like royalty there. Ronny and Patsy had a big house in the country, where I woke up every day to Patsy's hot honeybuns, eggs, bread, sausage, and bacon. After breakfast, my cousins and I went to the park or made up games in the backyard. We knocked down anthills and got bitten by the red ants. We spent a lot of time chucking fistfuls of Arkansas's famous red clay at each other until someone got hurt or we exhausted ourselves. One day I found a bicycle wheel, cut out the spokes, and nailed it to a tree. That became our basketball hoop. I learned to drive a tractor down there. Summertime in Arkansas was the best.

Sometimes we'd see my cousins from my granddad's side, who also lived in El Dorado. My great-grandmother—we called her Beebo—lived in a house on a hill that was really like a two-bedroom shack, every room at a slant. That place was *really* country, with dirt roads all through her neighborhood and roosters cock-a-doodle-dooing us awake each morning. Beebo's next-door neighbor sold penny candy. I didn't have to worry about a thing.

My family was religious. Back home in Minneapolis, Grandma Adams sent us kids to Sunday school each week, where we sang in the choir. The church community was "brother" this and "sister" that and became like a second family to us. After services, we went to visit Gramps's friends at the nursing home.

Actually, I attended two churches as a kid—one for each Grandma Shirley. Grandma Banks's church was Redeemer Missionary Baptist in South Minneapolis. That's where my parents got married. Grandma Adams went to First Church of God in Christ. That's where *I* got married. Later on, my great-uncle Freddy founded a nondenominational church called Fountain of Hope, where he served as the head pastor, with my uncle Rickey as assistant pastor. My aunts served as treasurer and secretary. I became one of the head deacons and chairman of the deacon board. I'm not sure why they decided to start their own church, but it was probably influenced by my great-grandfather on my mom's side, who was himself a deacon. His name was Jewel McGlothin, but he was Daddy Jewel to us. Daddy Jewel was a huge man—six-foot-five and three hundred pounds—with a deep voice and big glasses, always wearing a nice suit with suspenders. When it came to prayer and devotion, he was the best, a commanding presence. Once he got started, he would *go*. It was so powerful. Daddy Jewel made a point of trying to touch everybody in the church when he prayed, making each person feel like his prayer was personally delivered. It was a holy, physical feature of his fellowship. The man served the church almost until the day he died in 2020 at age ninety-two.

*   *   *

The Northside of Minneapolis has always been a place for marginalized communities. Until the 1950s, property ownership restrictions across most of the city forced large numbers of Blacks and Jews into the neighborhood. For the most part, everybody got along. By the 1960s, though, housing regulations had eased—for Jews, anyway—and many people moved to the suburbs. Things truly fractured in 1967, when discontent over the divergent paths of the neighborhood's residents—white folk moving up and out, Black folk staying stuck—boiled over. They say the trouble started when police manhandled a Black woman at the parade for the Minneapolis Aquatennial, an annual summer festival. It spurred a protest of angry citizens that wound its way into the heart of the neighborhood on Plymouth Avenue. Ten stores, mostly Jewish-owned, were looted or burned. Molotov cocktails were thrown at the home of a Jewish city councilman. The riot squad swooped in, followed by two hundred National Guard troops, as violence flared through the following week. Damage included eighteen fires, three shootings, thirtysix arrests, and a price tag of $4.2 million. After that, white residents couldn't get out fast enough. That left the Northside—our part of it, anyway—almost entirely Black.

My grandma Adams's house, where we lived when I was a baby, was half of a duplex, with me, my parents, my grandma, and my uncle Tony sharing two rooms. When my sister Brittney came along five years after me, the lot of us, Grandma included, moved to a place on Morgan Avenue, then to a bigger place at

Twenty-Second and Irving, just a few blocks from North High. Brittney and I shared a room upstairs. Downstairs were Grandma and Uncle Tony. We all made do with one bathroom. Dad and Grandpa fixed up the basement to include another bedroom, doing the framing, drywall, electrical, and plumbing themselves. I don't know how Dad found the time; he was a police officer by then.

I was eight years old, just the right age to begin exploring my new neighborhood. The Northside was filled with clapboard houses and plenty of swing sets in plenty of front yards. I quickly made friends with kids up and down the block. Ricky was three houses down. Robert was across the street from him. At the end of the block were Tong, Hin, and Ton on one side, and Donny and Jeff on the other. Lekon was around the corner. Across the street from me was Sean. Sean was white. So were Donny and Jeff. Tong, Hin, and Ton were Asian. Robert, Ricky, and Lekon were Black. That was our crew. For years, that's who I played with.

Our house was nice, with a backyard and a fence and a basketball hoop on the garage. It was in Minneapolis's poorest and most violent neighborhood, but us kids didn't pay much attention to that. We rode our bikes on a loop around the corner to Glen Gale Park and got our snacks at Tony's Market at the bottom of Irving and Broadway. Tony's is where my dad sent me on Sunday mornings to pick up a newspaper and a gallon of milk. The other place we went was the Big Stop on Twenty-Sixth, which they eventually tore down because there were so many murders there. It was such a gangbanger hangout that people were getting killed *inside* the store. I went there anyway because they sold jojo potatoes for $0.60 and three chicken wings for $1.25. For five bucks you could eat like a king at Big Stop.

Apart from those food runs, we pretty much never left the block. We played street football from the lamppost in front of my house to the one in front of the alley. We also played street basketball and street baseball and street hockey. When those lights came on, it was my cue to get back home. Even if I didn't notice it, I was always close enough to hear my mom call out from our front porch: "Spanky, the streetlights are on." That was the end of my day outdoors. Twenty-Second Avenue seemed so big to me then. When I drive through there now, it's small as hell.

Ricky was especially important because he introduced me to the Boys & Girls Club, which for a kid like me was the best thing ever. It was just a block away, on the other side of the park. Once we found it, all of us went there every chance we got. They had video games like *Pac-Man*, *Centipede*, and *Excitebike*, all for free. There was a beautiful indoor basketball court, Ping-Pong, foosball, and a swimming pool.

What stuck with me most was the drum corps.

I'd been playing drums since I was a kid, mainly at church services. I had a full Pearl kit with snare, toms, cymbals, and a beautiful maroon bass drum, and I ended up taking regular lessons at the Club. Those sessions became a lot more meaningful once Denny Green arrived.

When Dennis Green joined the Minnesota Vikings in 1992, he became only the second Black head coach in NFL history.

One of the first things he did in Minnesota was locate the Boys & Girls Club and, along with his wife, Marie, set up a sponsorship for us drummers. He'd been involved in his own local club as a kid, and I guess he wanted to pay it forward. Coach Green bought us drums and uniforms—Vikings polos and black pants—and arranged for us to perform at the team's home games as the Bus Green Music Team, named after his father. I'd been a crazy Vikings fan forever, and to say I was excited is an extreme understatement. I played with the Bus Green team all the way through high school. Coach Green and his wife treated us like we were their own kids, even inviting us to events at their house. Every time I saw Coach Green, he'd say, "There goes my drummer." If you find a copy of his autobiography, *No Room for Crybabies*, there's a photo on the back cover of Coach with a handful of his Music Team players. I'm in there, standing over his left shoulder.

Having a Black coach take over our hometown team didn't exactly get me thinking I'd be the next Dennis Green, mostly because I was still thinking I'd be the next Randy Moss. I was a football player long before I ever thought about coaching, and my dreams of glory all took place inside the lines. Years later, once I realized a playing career wasn't in my future, I found renewed inspiration from Coach Green. The widespread respect he commanded led me to wonder about becoming a football coach myself. I don't think a white coach, even one as generous as Dennis Green, would have had the same kind of impact. Seeing somebody who looked like me helping kids in our community made me want to be in that same position one day.

Through all the time he took with me and my friends, Coach Green showed me that coaching was about much more than sports. Today, for me, coaching high school kids has almost nothing to do with calling plays. I think that's why so many young coaches struggle. In their minds, they need the best schemes in order to be the best coaches. Well, I'm here to tell you that success doesn't have shit to do with your schemes. Success is about the connections you make and how you go about leading people. Success is getting kids to trust you, sometimes during their worst moments. Success is watching your players move on in their post-football lives, continuing to use the lessons you taught them on the field. I can't even count how many former players have told me about the straight line between high school football and the men they eventually became.

None of it had anything to do with the way I called a game.

For me, football was always a legacy sport. My father played in college. My first Peewee coach, Gary Wilson, was such a Northside institution that my dad played for him too, as a kid. When I was awarded a key to the city for leading North High to the 2016 Minnesota state championship, Coach Wilson presented it to me. I didn't have anything to do with that decision; it turned out the city was honoring him too.

Gary Wilson showed me what coaching could accomplish. He spent decades in our community, building a foundation of trust with our families through an amazing combination of honesty, availability, and good intentions. It wasn't only football. He was also my basketball coach, and he coached baseball during the spring. Coach Wilson would pick up kids who needed a ride to games or practices, and he went into his own pocket to make sure we had whatever equipment was necessary to compete. Some of my best memories with Coach Wilson involve detours he took to Dairy Queen on the way home after games to buy us all Blizzards.

Coach Wilson valued every player, not only the stars. Even when I was small, an eight-year-old playing on the ten-and-under team, I don't remember sitting on the bench because Coach emphasized that all his players had value somewhere. If I came to practice and did what I was supposed to do, I knew I'd be playing. As a coach myself, I hold that same ideal. I stayed with Coach Wilson for three years before moving up to Cubs, then Midgets, and finally to North High.

I was skinny as a kid, cautious, and not really tough, and I sometimes found myself bullied. In seventh grade I got into a fight with a way bigger classmate who pretty much beat me up just by pushing me around the locker room. I remember it mostly because I was fighting one-handed. A few weeks earlier I'd been hanging off the side of some spiral stairs at the YMCA, and when I let go, my ring—actually, it was my dad's class ring from North High—snagged on the edge and nearly yanked my finger off. When I looked down, I could see the tendon . . . until the blood started flowing. Oh, was there a lot of blood. They rushed me to the hospital, and it took doctors two hours just to cut the ring off my finger. My skin was shredded, the nerves wrecked. They had to more or less reconstruct the entire thing through grafts and surgery. It kept me out of football that season. I also had to have somebody help me write until I learned to manipulate a pencil with my left hand.

For months I wrapped my hand in bandages like a club, which might be why I punched that guy despite my injury. I don't think I hurt him, but I certainly set back my rehab. It wasn't much of a lesson. I kept right on fighting. Once my finger healed, I even got pretty good at it.

I liked living in our neighborhood, but the place kept getting sketchier and more violent. People moved out and slumlords bought up the houses, renting them to the wrong kinds of tenants. Before long, the potential for mayhem was off the charts. When I was thirteen I saw a guy shot to death at the corner of West Broadway and Irving. People broke into our detached garage and took Dad's lawnmower and my bike. On more than one occasion we had to hit the floor in the living room when we heard gunshots outside. I think the final straw came when I was in the front yard with my sister Brittney, who was five years younger than me, and my brother Styles, who was just a toddler. A lady pulled up and just like that began shooting. It was some sort of drive-by, and though it was focused on another house—she wasn't aiming at us—when you hear that noise, *pah-pah-pah-pah-pah*, you get low pretty damn quick.

From that moment, the clock was ticking on our time in that house. Dad was a stubborn Northsider who'd grown up in public housing and had built half of that house with his own hands. Nothing seemed to faze him. His police colleagues had been urging us to leave the neighborhood for a while. So had my mom. His kids almost getting shot, though? That had an effect. It was getting too crazy on our block, even for him.

We moved to a big house in a nicer Northside neighborhood, at Forty-First and Sheridan, just before I started tenth grade. That was also about the time my folks got divorced. Dad had been working a lot of jobs to make ends meet—full-time policing and part-time security gigs all over the place—and he tried to keep Mom happy with things like a new car every couple of years and an annual trip to Jamaica. He thought that was the hallmark of a good husband, but she obviously wanted more from the relationship. I was old enough by that point to see that they weren't happy together, and while I wasn't thrilled by the divorce, I at least understood why it was happening. For me, the hardest part was that Brittney and Styles went to live with Mom in a suburb about twenty minutes away. I stayed with my dad in the Northside because I didn't want to change schools. There wasn't even a debate. I heard Dad tell my mom, "You can take everything in this house, but Spanky stays." She took him up on that offer. Dad and I ended up loading virtually every piece of furniture we had into a moving truck. The only things left were our beds.

Our new house was just a few short blocks from Patrick Henry High School, an easy walk. Here's the thing, though: both my parents went to North, I'd spent my childhood thinking about how one day *I* would go to North, and I'd just finished my freshman year at North.

Patrick Henry is North's biggest rival.

So never mind that the house on Sheridan was virtually around the corner from Henry, and never mind that North High was three miles south along the Mississippi River. Never mind that Henry was *directly between* my home and North High. Was I gonna go to Patrick Henry?

Hell no.

That's our rival. They're the Patriots, and we're the Polars. To this day, the basketball competition between those schools is the craziest in Minneapolis. So instead of walking five minutes to school, I woke up forty-five minutes early, got my ass on the bus at 6:45 each morning, and found my way to the place I wanted to be.

I'd been looking forward to joining the Polars since my dad first brought me to the North High gym in the 1980s when I was four years old to watch my uncle Tony play on the basketball team. A while later, Dad helped coach JV basketball. We attended games there all the time. I was actually supposed to play freshman football for the Polars as an eighth grader, which a handful of kids do each year, but I'd missed my seventh-grade season with that finger injury and didn't think it was smart to jump straight from sixth-grade football into high school. So I waited.

During my freshman year, our varsity coach was a local legend named Mike Favor. A North High product himself, he won three Division II national championships as a center for North Dakota State University, earning enshrinement in the College Football Hall of Fame. Playing for Mike was like playing for a member of the family. He'd grown up in the projects with my dad, and was my uncle Tony's college roommate at NDSU. In a way, Mike owes his football career to my father. Dad never told me about it, but Mike did, years later.

Mike was a freshman at North when Dad was a senior, and though Mike had size—he was six-foot-one, 275 pounds—he didn't want to play football. Dad wouldn't have it. They knew each other from the neighborhood, and my father was determined. One day in the lunchroom he sidled over to Big Mike. "Football practice starts tomorrow," he said. "You better be there." Big Mike blew him off.

The way Mike tells it, the very next day Dad stormed up to him in the hallway. "I thought I told you to be at football practice yesterday," he said. Now my dad is put together, but he's regular-sized, not nearly as big as Mike. When Mike offered up some sort of excuse, Dad straight up punched him in the face. "Ima do this every day until you come to practice," he threatened. That did the trick. Mike showed up and never left. All of which meant I had a relationship with Coach Favor before I ever got to high school.

I played on the ninth-grade team my freshman year (we went undefeated), and my reward for knowing the coach was getting to suit up for the varsity squad and stand on the sideline for their games. I didn't play a snap until homecoming, when, in the middle of the game, one of the assistant coaches called for a volunteer. I didn't know what he wanted, and I didn't care. Before anyone could stop me, I ran onto the field. Us ninth graders ran the same playbook as the varsity team, so I knew I'd recognize whatever play was called. It turned out that they needed a holder for the placekick. It wasn't much of a role, but I wasn't complaining. We were at the ten-yard line, and the snap ended up flying right over my head. I was quick enough to leap and catch it, then wheeled right and threw it to my boy Marcus Ross in the back of the end zone. A touchdown pass. At homecoming. As a freshman. On my first-ever play. Yeah, that was a rush.

As a side note, I mentioned before that my family nickname is Spanky. Well, so is Coach Favor's, so he became Big Spank and I became Little Spank. Coach always thought my dad nick-named me after him, which Dad never argued with, even though it wasn't true. Big Spank ended up working in the school district for decades, eventually becoming a superintendent.

I played JV my sophomore year and was in line to make the full-time jump to varsity as a junior. That season was shaping up to be monumental. Coach Favor had taken an administra-tion job at nearby St. Louis Park High, and Rufus Bess stepped in to coach. For me, it was hard to believe—when I was a kid, Rufus Bess had been a star defensive back with the Vikings, one of my favorite players. I couldn't wait to get onto the field with that guy.

I ran into a roadblock, though. More accurately, I built myself a roadblock, and then ran into it.

Mom moving out of the house had given me newfound freedom. I was sixteen, with a driver's license and a father who was constantly at work, leaving me all kinds of unsupervised time. It didn't help that Dad's hobby was buying old cars and fixing them up, just like his father had done before him. As a kid, I spent a lot of time at the scrapyard with Dad and Pawpaw, playing around in junked vehicles while they hunted for automotive treasure. There was *always* a car available at our house. My first, which Dad gave me shortly after I got my license, was a 1991 Mercury Topaz. I made a point of driving around the whole of Minneapolis, making sure people saw me. After that came a two-door Chevy Cavalier, and then a Ford Explorer. I got to drive them all, right up until Dad sold them. The Explorer was especially sweet because it was nearly new. It had been in a wreck—that's why it was at the junkyard—but I sure turned some heads when I took that thing around town.

Dad had some motivation to keep me with a ride because I was able to pick up and drop off my siblings from the suburbs when they spent weekends at our house. He also used those cars as incentive, starting the moment I got my license. Tying his vehicles to my grades was powerful motivation. It took me all of one day to learn just how powerful.

Dad gave me that Mercury when I got my license, but the very next day he needed to drive it to work. For some long-forgotten reason, he left the Mercury at the police station and brought his work car home, forcing me to ride the bus one more day. It wouldn't have been a big deal had that not also been the day grades came out. North High was a magnet school, with kids assigned to the arts-and-communications unit or the math-and-science unit. Math and science were my worst subjects, but that's where I ended up. My grades reflected as much. Dad saw my progress report that night and laid down the law.

"Put your keys on the table and leave them there," he said. I couldn't believe it. I got to drive my Mercury one fucking day, and I wouldn't get it back until my grades improved.

As it turned out, that was just a prelude to what was to come. The next thing Dad took away would be far more painful.

Chapter 2

Gridiron to Gumshoe

I had the same dream as every guy on the North High football team: go on to play college ball, and then to the NFL. In my neighborhood, though, options were slim. The University of Minnesota is only fifteen minutes away, yet for reasons none of us understood, they never recruited our players. We were a poor Black school in a poor Black neighborhood, and I guess the folks at UM viewed us all as thugs. Well, my teammates went on to be pastors and business owners and corporate managers and even an executive for a multinational corporation. Plus at least one cop.

To me, the crazy part is that nothing has changed. As a North High coach, I gave the Golden Gophers their all-time leading receiver, Tyler Johnson, and he ended up there almost by accident, recruited by UM only after Big Ten rivals Iowa and Wisconsin made him offers. (After an outstanding collegiate career from 2016 to 2019, Tyler went on to win a Super Bowl ring with the Tampa Bay Buccaneers, catching passes from Tom Brady.) As I write this in 2023, I have a former player at Nebraska who's going to be an All-American and will probably be selected in the top four rounds of the NFL draft, and another kid at Penn State. In all, seven of my guys are currently playing Division I football. If you were a football recruiter for the University of Minnesota, why the hell *wouldn't* you come to my school every damn year when you're literally minutes away? Honestly, for all those years, if the Gophers' head coach was blindfolded, spun around a few times, and instructed to walk to North High, he'd have no idea which way to go. If I sound angry about this, it's because I am.

North High kids are perpetually shortchanged. I have athletes with 4.0 GPAs and good test scores, and we win state championships or come damn close just about every year. That isn't enough to obscure the fact that our student body is 97 percent minority and 90 percent Black. Sixty-seven percent of our kids are economically disadvantaged, but somehow most local scholarships seem to fly toward well-off families at suburban schools. I can't say it's purely racial because plenty of Black athletes get those scholarships—just not *my* Black athletes. And when I was in high school, it sure as hell wasn't me.

North High is in the middle of the roughest part of Minneapolis. When other teams see North on their schedule, they inevitably ask, "Which one—the hood North or the other North?" The other North High is in St. Paul. It doesn't take much to figure out which one they want to visit.

Once college recruiters run out of reasons to avoid us, their final dagger is that North Community High School is too small.

Even after winning the state championship in 2016, we kept hearing how we only play Class A. (In Minnesota, the largest schools are in the 6A division.) The year we took the title, our enrollment was about 430. Never mind that I always schedule bigger schools during our regular season, and never mind that we almost always beat them. When it comes to the state tournament, recruiters hold our small student body size against us. At that point, there's not much I can do.

As for my own collegiate aspirations, I pretty much ended them on my own, before UM or anybody else could get around to ignoring me. By the end of my sophomore year of high school I was spending most of my time hanging out with friends and trying to get with girls. My group called ourselves the Naughty Nine, and while there actually were nine of us, we were anything but naughty. Some of us played football at North, some played basketball, some did both. We were all in student council, members of citywide student government, and in a group called Drug-Free Athletes. The most trouble we got into was when we stole hall passes to crash a yearbook photo session, then convinced the photographer that the Naughty Nine was a legitimate school club. It worked; our picture actually showed up in the yearbook, although the photographer must have misheard us when we identified ourselves because we're listed as the "Ninety-Nines." Oh well.

If the Naughty Nine had any sort of negative influence on me, it's that I preferred spending time with them to doing schoolwork. I also had access to an automobile and freedom to roam the streets at $1.50 a gallon. By the end of the year I'd

compiled enough Cs and Ds to drag my GPA below the 2.0
minimum required to play football the following fall. I could
still practice with the team, but I was ineligible to dress for
games. When my dad found out, he just about flipped. How he
found out didn't help.

The Minneapolis City Conference ran something called
previews, a mash-up of preseason scrimmages within a single
event, where each local team played a quarter against another
team, allowing everybody to take a look at all the competition.
It was a combination showcase and dress rehearsal. My dad
took off work early to see us and found me on the sideline in
regular clothes. When I explained to him why I wasn't playing,
he didn't miss a beat. "Let's go," he said and dragged me to the
car. We drove home in uncomfortable silence. When we got
inside, Dad put out his hand. "Car keys." Oh shit. "Pager." I
handed over the goods. That man confiscated every fringe benefit of my teenage life. He yelled about how badly I'd fucked up,
how stupid I'd been to lose focus on my schoolwork, and what a
steep price I'd pay for that lapse. I quickly longed for the silence
of the car ride home.

I'm sure part of Dad's anger came from embarrassment.
Charles Adams's son was not supposed to suffer from laziness
or bad grades. Having to bus to school again was one thing, but
I'd been responsible for picking up my brother and sister from
across town, and Dad even took that away, saying he'd rather do
it himself than let me anywhere near a car. From that point forward I came home directly from practice—on the bus, of course.
No more hanging out with friends.

The most frustrating part was still to come. Not long thereafter, I learned that I could appeal the school's decision to keep me off the team. I hadn't failed any classes, my attendance was good, and I'd only barely missed that 2.0. I had friends who'd appealed longer-shot circumstances than mine, and they'd been reinstated. All I needed was to pledge that my grades would improve, and Dad had to sign the form.

He wouldn't do it. Even if the school was willing to let me play, Officer Adams wasn't.

If only it ended there. A week or two after previews, he dropped one more punishment on me. "Since you can't help the team by playing football, you'll help in another way," he said. "Take your ass onto that field and wipe them balls off for the players. You're going to be the ball boy this season." Oh shit, anything but that. I tried to talk him out of it, but Dad had already arranged it with Coach Favor. I was now the guy running in from the sideline during pauses in the action to bring water to players. It was downright humiliating. Punishing me by taking away football was one thing. Making me face my peers in shame on a weekly basis was next level.

It worked. My friends in the Naughty Nine could not believe I was missing the football season because I failed to maintain a C average. I had no retort; they were right. I even came close to getting kicked out of the group. My friend Javonte said, "Man, if you can't get your grades, you can't fool with us." That was some motivation right there. Those guys came through for me, though, doing whatever they could to make sure my GPA was where it needed to be. Then, after they finished helping, they ran my ass ragged on that sideline. "Bring me some water." "Wipe my face." "Take this towel." Abuse the ball boy, just because they could. I took it because I had no choice. Also, it's what I deserved. Javonte is one of my best friends to this day.

As hard-assed as my dad was, I had a hard time resenting him for it. Dad *loved* football, yet it was still an easy decision for him. I might even have received a college scholarship had I suited up my junior year, but Dad needed to show me that academics were the most important thing. He doubled down by making me read a bunch of Hooked on Phonics books each Saturday morning in addition to my regular schoolwork. I'd like to say that his punishments steered me right, but they didn't hold nearly the power of not being able to play sports. I should have been starring on that North High team, and instead I was wiping down the damn balls.

I made certain that by the time basketball season rolled around my grades were good enough to play. It's not like there was any kind of party at my house once I regained eligibility. Dad wasn't about to celebrate a 2.0. That had been his minimum expectation all along. At least I got my car back, mostly so I could resume picking up my siblings from across town.

Now that I'm a coach myself, I'm reminded of Dad's lessons whenever a player's grades suffer. Just like Dad, I have refrained from signing off on appeals that might allow guys to play with substandard GPAs. Kids sometimes turn to an assistant coach in hopes of finding an ally to convince me otherwise. Sometimes that coach is my father. Dad thinks it's hilarious. "Why don't you go ask what happened his junior year?" he'll instruct.

When players hear that story, they stop asking. The reason Dad wouldn't do it for me is the same reason I won't do it for them: academics are the most important thing.

When it came to grades, my final trick arrived at the end of my senior year at North High. Our graduation program listed academic achievements next to each student's name—things like honor roll and the National Honor Society. Well, in that program *all* of them were listed next to my name, every recognition, title after title. Dad didn't buy it for a second. "What the fuck is this?" he asked. "Everybody's congratulating me on your academics, and you barely made it through. Did you pay somebody to put all of this in there?" Come on, Dad. Can't you give me even a little credit?

But yeah, it was all bogus. Honestly, I have no idea how it happened. They might have accidentally copied the stats from my friend Javonte, whose name was just below mine. I might not have been as great as the program said, but I ended up doing okay.

When my senior season started, I felt like I had to prove everything to everyone after wasting the previous year on the sideline. I made the most of my opportunity to play for Coach Bess, becoming an All-Conference tight end with the best hands on the team. During a game against Cretin-Derham Hall High School, I ate up a free safety named Joe Mauer for 103 yards on four receptions, my best game ever. Mauer, who went on to become an All-Star catcher and American League MVP for the Minnesota Twins, wasn't the only stud on that defense. Playing alongside him was Matt Birk, who soon would be starring for the Vikings and the Ravens. Years later, Matt told me he still remembers how I ran through them that day.

That was a good season for North. We went 5–1 and beat our crosstown rival, Patrick Henry High, in the annual Northside Championship game. Actually, to call Henry our rival isn't quite accurate. The school is only three miles up Penn Avenue, but it's almost like we were playing different sports. The final score was 77–0, on their field no less. How bad was it? We didn't throw the ball once. I was our star tight end and didn't have a catch. We were so happy after the game, but Coach Bess wouldn't let us have it. Not at first. "Y'all better put your helmets on to walk to the bus," he said as soon as the whistle sounded. We were like, "What? We want everybody to see us." Sure enough, as soon as we started to move, people began throwing small rocks at us. *Tink. Tink.* I guess Coach Bess was right. In my fourteen years as a coach I've lost to Henry only once, back in my third season. The rivalry includes a traveling trophy, held by the defending victor, and I am determined they will never get it back. That isn't much of a problem these days since Henry refuses to play us anymore, despite being in a bigger division. (Did having rocks thrown at us teach me any lessons about running up the score? It did not. Not against Henry, anyway. If we ever play them again, I want to put a thousand points up on that scoreboard.)

The most lasting lesson of my senior year was the realization that sitting out the previous season screwed up whatever opportunities I might have had to play at the next level. One by one my teammates were signed by colleges, but those conversations never materialized for me. The only recruiters I spoke with were on campus to meet my teammates, and I just went along for the ride. The only program to show real interest in me was the University of Minnesota Morris, an NCAA Division III school about two-and-a-half hours west of Minneapolis. DIII schools don't offer scholarships, though, and without financing I couldn't afford it.

It didn't take long to realize I needed a backup plan. Luckily, North High hosted a career fair. Among the participants was the Minneapolis Police Department.

Dad was a cop, of course, working in homicide by that point. I was aware of how difficult his journey had been. He'd paid out of pocket to attain a law-enforcement certificate he couldn't afford, and once he had it nobody was hiring. Dad was one of twelve hundred people to apply for forty positions with the Hennepin County Sheriff's Office. He didn't get the job. He applied to the State Patrol and to the St. Paul PD. Not a sniff. He finally hooked on with the Minneapolis Police Department. Today, fewer than twenty people apply for those kinds of jobs, half of them without even meeting the minimum requirements. Times have changed.

At the job fair I learned that if I committed to becoming an officer, the police department would pay for my schooling, so that became my plan. I couldn't wait to get home and tell Dad about it.

He was 100 percent not on board.

Dad knew the racial politics of policing in Minneapolis, understood what it was like to be Black and wear blue, not only in the community but within the department, and he wanted to save me from that. His brother Tony had also ended up with the MPD and encountered similar hurdles. Instead, Dad urged me to go to barber school. I'd been cutting hair—his, my granddad's, my brother's, my uncles'—since I was thirteen. Dad wanted me to open my own shop.

I didn't want to be a barber. I wanted to be a cop.

That my dad rose to the rank of inspector in the Minneapolis Police Department is a testament to his strength and perseverance. Before he even began training, a sergeant said he'd never make it because he was "too Black." On the third day of Dad's first assignment, he and his supervising officer nabbed a guy wanted in a triple murder without so much as firing a shot. One of the homicide investigators wrote up Dad and his trainer for an award, but the precinct captain denied it, claiming the MPD didn't give awards to rookies . . . even as other rookies received commendations. Did it have anything to do with the fact that both cops in question were African American?

Here's a prime example of the kind of crap Dad faced. As an officer, he earned a master's of human resources degree from Concordia University in St. Paul, along with a fellow officer named Medaria Arradondo. Years later, Arradondo was promoted to head of internal affairs and asked Dad to transfer over with him. Dad was all for it, but instead the position went to a less qualified white guy. It took only a couple of months for the department to realize Black citizens simply weren't opening up to a white person asking them questions, at which point Chief Janeé Harteau—the person who'd passed Dad over in the first place—circled back and fast-tracked him for the job. The assistant chief, Kris Arneson, asked Chief Harteau why she hadn't selected Dad the first time around. The chief's answer: "I heard he has poor writing skills."

Oh, for fuck's sake.

"Chief, Charlie has a master's degree," Kris pointed out. Not only that, but Dad had earned that master's alongside Arradondo, the guy who recommended him for the job. The chief hadn't known that, and didn't bother to find out. Stereotypes reign. All's well that ends well, I guess—that job was one in a string of promotions for Dad that led to his serving as inspector of the Fourth Precinct, just a rung down from chief.

Dad came up with a handful of Black officers—Malcolm Long, Larry Wakefield, and Monte Manning, comprising Squad 530—as his departmental mentors. He worked the B shift, from 7 p.m. to 2 a.m., with another group of mostly Black officers—Johnny Carter, Melvin Adams (no relation), plus one white guy, Richard Zimmerman. In those days, almost all the department's African American officers were bunched together in a single precinct. They were a solid unit . . . until one of their white colleagues played a joke by planting dope in the steering wheel of their patrol car, along with a note that read, "Catch me now."

The department had been running a drug probe of its officers for more than two years, and this was enough to spur an internal affairs investigation into every one of those guys, Dad included. It's almost like top brass was looking for an excuse. Talk about implicit bias. Malcolm drove a Mercedes. Dad's partner, Johnny Carter, drove a Chevy Blazer with a souped-up sound system. Dad drove a Cadillac and carried a pager. They wore gold chains. Of *course* the white cops in Special Investigations thought the Black guys were dealing dope—they couldn't tell the difference between Black style and drug-dealer style.

Back then, Black cops were more popular in Minneapolis than the Vikings. They went to the hippest nightspots, got valet parking, and didn't have to stand in line. That's how much respect they had. When police investigators trailed them into clubs, they figured Dad and the boys must be doing something dirty. Well, they weren't doing anything besides having a good time while Black.

It didn't help that the sergeant in charge of Special Investigations was a stone-cold racist. He did plenty of work investigating white cops who were actually dirty, but the guy was pulling down so much money in overtime pay that he was more than happy to investigate Dad and the guys, too, even without compelling evidence. How do I know he was racist? He informed people that Dad was flying to Bogotá, Colombia, and bringing back dope, even though Dad had never been farther from home than his annual trip to Arkansas. Somehow, every cop investigated in this bogus scheme was Black (plus one Native American), while Zimmerman, the white member of the group—who ended up becoming Dad's partner in the homicide division for many years—didn't get so much as a sniff.

Those investigators surveilled Dad and his friends for months, digging through their garbage, treating them like *they* were the criminals. Dad didn't even know it was happening.

You might ask whether the whole thing could have been avoided if the cop who'd planted the drugs in the first place simply came out and admitted it was all a joke. Well, he might have done that had he known what was going on, but the investigation was secret, and he didn't realize his prank was being taken seriously until it was too late.

Here's what "too late" looks like: one day, Larry went to lunch at Sunny's, a Minneapolis restaurant popular with African Americans, and encountered an MPD SWAT team outside. He was on duty, in full uniform, and asked if they needed help with their assignment. It turned out that their assignment was Larry. As they put him under arrest, one of those pricks actually pointed his MP5 submachine gun at his head before they cuffed him and took him downtown.

Another bust was staged at another restaurant Dad and his Black colleagues frequented, Jose's Old Southern Barbecue. Investigators cited officers being spotted there talking to a low-level drug dealer. Nobody claimed they'd bought or sold drugs—only talked to the guy. It's as if they had no idea that's how street-level connections work.

Dad found out about the Jose's bust when his partner, John Carter, called him, trying to make sense of it all. "Shit, Johnny, it's almost like they were looking for *us*," Dad told him. "Those are the places *we* go." In the middle of that conversation, Dad heard John's doorbell ring. "Uh oh," Johnny told him, "the inspector's here."

With that, they got Johnny, too. In the middle of the phone call.

Dad contacted his lawyer, and a meeting was arranged downtown with the deputy chief. That's when Dad first saw the case file the department had been building on him for over a year. It was three inches thick.

Dad's attorney blew every accusation out of the water. Even the deputy chief said something didn't smell right. Dad ended up exonerated, but Johnny and Melvin lost their jobs on trumped-up department policy violations. Johnny had a mouth on him and once told a lieutenant to go fuck himself, so it's not hard to see why they had it out for him. An undercover officer even tried to lure Johnny into selling her cocaine, which he didn't do because he wasn't a drug dealer. They never pressed criminal charges against him, probably because they had no evidence to substantiate them. Wakefield didn't lose his job, but the investigation triggered the PTSD he'd developed while serving in Vietnam, and he had to take medical leave. He never returned. Overall, the MPD's internal drug probe led to the dismissal of thirteen officers, eight of them Black. For Dad's friends, it left a burning feeling. Their own colleagues had done this to them.

All these details went into Dad's response when I first told him I wanted to join the force. I can sum up what he said in three words: "Don't do it." (I can sum it up in four words if we include expletives.) He knew just how difficult it was for a Black cop to make it, and he wanted to save me from the kind of racist crap he'd faced.

Dad was not only one of the prominent Black voices on the force, but *the* prominent Black voice, and had been almost since the day he'd arrived. My father is outspoken and polarizing when it comes to race relations. Diversity in recruitment is his thing. He's a guy who, if you're wrong, will tell you you're wrong, and it doesn't matter who you are. He's been through eight chiefs so far and has got on every one of their asses—respectfully, of course—when it came to communities of color. Dad's outspokenness has made him a few enemies along the way. He figured that a lot of cops would count it as a strike against me when they found out I was Charlie Adams's kid. He wasn't wrong.

Ultimately, Dad barely helped me in the early going. I guess he figured if I was going to make it, I had to do it on my own. By the time I took my assessment test, Dad realized it was inevitable. I was going to be a cop, and there was nothing he could do to dissuade me. He decided to support me fully.

Chapter 3

FTOutrage

I was that kid who, whenever I saw a cop car in the neighborhood, would run up to it with a smile on my face. Unlike most kids, of course, I got to shout, "Hey, do you know my dad?" I also asked after the football cards they sometimes passed out as community outreach. McGruff the Crime Dog was on those cards, which turned some kids off, but so were the Vikings, and to me nothing else mattered. "I already got Joey Browner and Carl Lee and Rufus Bess and John Swain—do you have a Chris Doleman?" (Not only did Bess become my high school coach, but my first-ever win when I took over the North program was against John Swain, who was coaching at Patrick Henry. Talk about rubbing elbows with your heroes.)

All of which is a long way of saying I've always liked the police. When they agreed to pay for my schooling, I liked them even more.

I stayed in the neighborhood, enrolling at North Hennepin Community College, then finished my law-enforcement
degree nearby, at Minneapolis Community and Technical College. As part of the deal for the department covering my tab, I
also worked part-time as a community service officer, an entry-
level administrative position that made me feel like a cop, even
though I was mostly a gofer. CSOs did things like pick up mail,
order supplies, get the cars washed, and make inter-precinct
deliveries. I was given an official MPD uniform, which was cool.
I didn't get a gun, but I was allowed to drive a squad car and felt
like part of the team.

Working twenty hours per week while handling a full course
load was not easy. Thankfully, I had a girlfriend who offered
plenty of emotional support. I'd met Andreaua Kennedy (who
everybody knew as Peanut, then and now) years earlier, but she'd
since moved out to the suburbs. Thankfully, her cousin was my
friend and North High football teammate Marcus Owens, and
she came down to watch one of our games. I saw Andreaua and
one of her friends waiting for Marcus outside the locker room
and went over to flirt. Unfortunately, the person I flirted with
was her friend. I didn't have much choice—the girl gave me a
big hug and a kiss on the cheek. Teenage boys don't need much
more motivation than that.

Later that night my friend Toki pulled me aside. "I saw Peanut at the game," he said, "and she told me to pass her number
along to you." Heck, I'd just got done trying to holler at her
friend, but this was good news. I'd had a crush on Andreaua
since I first saw her at a seventh-grade dance at Franklin Middle

School. She was such a great dancer that I pretty much just stood back and watched her. I called that number in a hurry. That was 1999, and we've been together ever since.

Andreaua was smart and beautiful, with black hair and gorgeous eyes. She was fun and loved sports. It was a haul for me to get out to Maple Grove, where she'd moved, but she was worth it. Her parents had a big house with room enough for Andreaua, her brother and sisters, her niece and nephew, and even her grandmother. It was a world away from living alone with my dad. I spent a lot of time that year in Maple Grove.

Andreaua ended up going to North Hennepin Community College with me, and then to nursing school. Along the way, she got pregnant. Our son, Adrian, was born in 2000, and our first daughter, Anyla, came four years later. In between, we got married. (I didn't want a wedding until I had a job, and I wouldn't have a real job until I graduated from the academy.) I spent all my money on a ring, and then we had a very long engagement.

Telling Dad my girlfriend was pregnant was not easy. He'd done the same thing at my age and had specifically warned me against it. Dad was less angry than realistic. The first thing out of his mouth was, "Man, you just made things a lot harder on yourself." Yeah, Dad knew what he was talking about. I was nineteen years old, the same age he had been when I was born. He raised me while going to school and working a lot of part-time hours to pay the bills. None of it had been easy.

Dad was right. I was a college student, and suddenly I had to pay for a baby and a two-bedroom apartment in Brooklyn Park. Rent was $800 a month, and I was making $12.50 an hour as a

CSO, twenty hours per week. I earned extra cash working loss prevention at Sears—I was effectively a non-uniformed security guard—for another twenty hours each week. We lived paycheck to paycheck, which sometimes left enough money for gas or diapers, but not both. Which to choose? I didn't want to ask my father for help. I'd seen him work all kinds of off-duty gigs to bring in extra money for our family, and I was supporting my own family now. I had to do this on my own.

Since Toki is the guy who handed me Andreaua's number, this seems like a good place to talk about him. Well, not about Toki himself, although he remains one of my good friends, but to illustrate the kind of impact a community can have on a kid. In high school, Toki's girlfriend got pregnant, and he did the honorable thing by moving in with her and her mom to help care for the baby. A belated paternity test, however, showed that the child wasn't his. Well, so much for living in *that* house. Toki's mother had moved to Nebraska by that point, and his dad was pretty much out of the picture, leaving Toki effectively homeless.

Well, me and my dad were all alone in that big house at 41st and Sheridan, and when I asked if Toki could move in, it wasn't even a question. Of course he could. If there's one thing to know about my dad, it's that he takes care of people. Toki ended up staying with us for two years—his senior year of high school and his freshman year at the University of Minnesota, which he attended through a program designed for inner-city kids. Toki was a rapper and was constantly leaving sheets of lyrics all over the place. College was a great opportunity for him, and he stuck with it. He eventually became department head of the country's first fully accredited, degree-offering hip-hop studies program, at McNally Smith College of Music in St. Paul, then went on to chair the professional music department at the Berklee College of Music in Boston. Toki Wright is a literal professor of hip-hop.

Would any of that have happened if Dad hadn't opened up our home to Toki, charged him no rent, and let him eat our food? There's no way to know. What's certain is that Toki is now heavily invested in community service while keeping an eye out for our neighborhood from afar, not to mention the example he sets for every kid who comes from the same place he did. Anything is possible.

To advance to the police academy in Minneapolis, recruits must pass an eight-week skills course at the Center for Criminal Justice and Law Enforcement, which looks a lot like college with an intense focus on police work. While I sailed through hands-on topics like patrol ops and defensive tactics, I found the class on statutes and codes to be mystifying. Between my full-time college schedule, my part-time CSO workload, and a baby at home, I never seemed to find the time necessary to grasp the rote memorization it required. Through my entire college education, it's the only class I ever struggled in. I ended up failing and had to retake it at nighttime while I took my next course load during the day. At least my second time through was smoother than the first. I'd already taken the class, which helped, but mostly it was because my new teacher was more invested in my success. Really, it was as simple as a single hint he offered. The first time around I'd nearly killed myself trying to memorize every statute in the damn book, but my new instructor had me focus primarily on the 609 criminal code, which covers the vast majority of police work. That made things much more manageable.

At the end, the only thing standing between me and the academy was a fitness test—a mile-and-a-half run that had to be completed in under fourteen minutes and forty-three seconds. I weighed about 250 pounds at that point, thirty above my high school playing weight—in decent shape but not at all fast. I'd passed the same test to get into the academy, so I knew I could do it, and I was astounded when my time didn't come close to qualifying. My fitness must really have lapsed while I was focused on all that classwork.

Somehow, nobody told me that I'd be disqualified if I didn't pass that part. The only reason I didn't show up at the academy for what would have been my first day was because a friend of my dad's, an officer in the recruitment program named Lisa Davis, warned me against it. Through Lisa, I got my first taste of the various factions working against my success. We talked on a Thursday. My first day at the academy was supposed to be a few days later, on the following Monday.

"Charles, they *want* you to show up so they can tell you in front of everybody that you're not supposed to be there," Lisa told me. "They want to publicly send you away and embarrass you."

The "they" Lisa was talking about were two people: the cadre officer—the trainer—and his sergeant. Perhaps their intent was to throw shade at Dad and Uncle Tony, who by that point was a patrolman himself, for being so outspoken about diversity on the force. Or maybe it was because I was one of two Black recruits in a class of twenty, which made me an easy target for some latent racism from the top. There's a good-old-boy network inside the MPD, just like at police departments across the country.

The consequence was that I was sent back to recruitment for another sixty days, my only requirement being to work on my running. I had one more chance at that mile-and-a-half; if I didn't complete it quickly enough, my police career would be over before it began. Talk about pressure. I kept thinking about it like I would a football game: it was the end of the fourth quarter, and I needed a touchdown to win. The trick was figuring out how to get it. I spent two solid months working out with my CSO sergeant, Melissa Banham, who sweated almost as much as I did trying to get my time down. After sixty days I tried again.

The distance was composed of twelve laps around the indoor track at the Northwest Athletic Club, where the academy did its training. I set a goal of one minute per lap but couldn't quite keep up with it. When I reached that final circuit, Melissa gave me my time: thirteen minutes. It was slower than I wanted, but it still gave me a minute and forty-three seconds to push one last time around the track. This sounds like hyperbole, but it's the absolute truth: my entire career hinged on that happening. I was tired and my back was killing me, but I burned it out. Melissa was cheering so hard her voice cracked. I guess I wasn't the only nervous one.

When I turned onto the last straightaway, I kicked into another gear. I felt like Usain Bolt, going a hundred miles per hour. When I watched the video later, I couldn't believe the difference between how fast I felt and how slow I looked, but I managed to cross the finish line with almost thirty seconds to spare. Melissa's response was someplace between happiness and relief.

I did it. I got it. I was on my way.

The Minneapolis Police Academy offered a sixteen-week intensive program on how to be a cop: things like policies and procedures, patrol operations, and city logistics. They labeled it the "Minneapolis Way." We trained on the field and at the firing range. The program wasn't residential, so I got to go home to my family each night. After my previous coursework, it was a breeze.

One hardship my delay caused was financial. As a policeman, you are given a uniform stipend to purchase your own equipment, but CSOs are not afforded that privilege. This meant shelling out for a whole lot of gear. Pants were $80 per pair, and I needed three. Shirts were another $70. There were boots and jogging pants. We even had to buy our own MPD insignia patches at $3 a pop. It added up to more than $500 worth of stuff. The rest of the necessary equipment—gun, gun belt, magazine, and a whole mess more—carried its own impossible price tag. My pistol—a .40-caliber Beretta 92FS—cost $600. My bulletproof vest was $1,300. All told, I had to lay out thousands of dollars just to suit up.

The rest of my class of 2004 had graduated while I was busy running, so I had a private swearing-in ceremony in the chief's office—just my dad, my wife, and our young son, plus assorted friends and family members. The city clerk came in, and I raised my hand and recited my oath. Chief McManus handed a badge to my grandmother, who pinned it onto my shirt.

Finally. Let's get to work.

My final piece of training consisted of five one-month periods, each with a different patrol officer. It's standard fare, and for many officers the experience wouldn't be worth recounting. In my case it is, for reasons that enrage me to this day.

Things started out fine. I reported to the Third Precinct for my first shift, middle-watch, from 4 p.m. to 2 a.m. My job was to follow the lead of my field training officer, otherwise known as an FTO. He graded me on a five-point scale for things like officer safety, report readiness, and command presence. A passing score was required to advance to the next month's assignment. The end of those five months included a ten-day trial during which I'd patrol more or less by myself, accompanied by a plainclothes officer whose primary job was to watch me work. After that I could finally roll solo—what we call "able"—as a full-fledged officer.

The first phase of field training is mostly intended to intro-
duce recruits to the department. You're brand new, and expectations are moderate. Mostly it's about getting a feel for the flow
of police work. The problem with the FTO system is that the
framework of policing is not designed for learning. In fact, it's
the opposite of that—it's set up for failure. The field training
struggles encountered by many recruits stem from the fact that
cops aren't teachers, they're cops. If you can't figure things out on
your own, as often as not the guy training you will simply assume
you're no good at those things. You make it or you're done.

My first FTO was a SWAT officer named Billy Jack Peter-
son. He was a good guy, squared away, and gave me my first real
lessons about police work. Billy Jack made sure I knew exactly
why I'd been given every grade I received, and that I understood
what I needed to do to improve. The first thing he taught me
was how to thoroughly search a suspected drug dealer, which
includes putting your fingers in sensitive areas.

My second month was spent with a different officer, also in
the Third Precinct, who tossed me to the departmental wolves.
Under her, everybody on the shift took to loading me up with
report-writing jobs. She never turned anybody down. Because
you're not allowed to write a report without having been at the
scene, I found myself fielding a constant stream of Code 4s—
on-scene situations where no backup is required—just so the cop
on hand could offload his report-writing onto me. That's not an
unusual practice with rookies, but with this FTO it happened
all the time. Simple reports took between thirty and forty-five

minutes, and things like DWIs and domestic assaults up to two hours. I found myself saddled with four or five reports a night, which basically ate up my entire shift. Our radio was constantly crackling with requests for my FTO: "Hey, does your recruit want to take this call?" The answer was always yes. Other than report writing, I hardly learned a thing about police work that month. Still, that FTO wasn't a bad cop. She wasn't what's known as a "load"—people who avoid work at all costs, looking the other way when calls go out, content to do the bare minimum to make things easier on themselves. For me, the load came next.

When my primary FTO was off duty, I rode with a guy named James, who wasn't a field training officer and didn't want to be. As far as I could tell, James's sole purpose as a cop was to get home safely. I know this because he told me as much. "I don't give a shit about your scores and your evaluation," he said the first day we met. "Just don't get me killed."

Safety is important, but the way James presented it messed me up. It was almost like suggesting that I would put him in harm's way. It was insulting.

James didn't give a shit about quality police work. He didn't do a lick of proactive policing. We responded to the 911 calls that were routed directly to us, and nothing more. This guy was happy to sit in the precinct and play computer games, or park on a side street and watch movies on his portable DVD player. I mean, lots of us watched movies during quiet moments of an overnight shift, but this guy took time from necessary policing to lay as low as possible. I literally watched him pause a movie when a call came over the radio. "Somebody else can get that," he said, and then he went right back to his screen. James was one lazy motherfucker.

Another officer I rode with was Justin. What I appreciate most about him had to do with my daughter, Anyla. She was born early, at twenty-four weeks, just before I began my FTO training. She weighed one pound, thirteen ounces and spent her first four months of life in neonatal intensive care. Thankfully, the hospital was also in the Third Precinct, so I could be with her during the day and have only a short trip to work that evening. Better still, Justin pulled me aside shortly after our first assignment and gave me an order: "Every shift you have, you better go down to that hospital and see your daughter." Then he backed it up. Every time we worked together, Justin would park the car at the hospital during our forty-five-minute meal breaks and wait while I went upstairs. (To be fair, James also occasionally went to the hospital with me, mostly because it allowed him to nap while I was with my family.)

FTO training shifts from precinct to precinct, and I knew my third month would be in the Fourth Precinct. The Northside. My neighborhood. Oh, how I looked forward to patrolling those streets.

My first FTO in the Fourth was a cop named Joe Schany, who I ended up working with later as a full-time patrolman. Joe was great. He got his recruits involved in everything, and he would not let me fail. Whenever I had trouble with something, we'd go over it again and again until I got it right. That's especially impressive in a place like the Fourth, the most dangerous part of town, where things can get intense. Joe set the foundation for me when it came to responsible police work.

My fourth of five phases was also in the Fourth Precinct, the overnight dog watch under a cop named Scott Taylor. If Joe was great, Scott was phenomenal. One story illustrates how focused he was on improving my policing. The two of us were on a domestic assault call, checking out a report of a guy beating up his girlfriend at Twenty-Fourth and Bryant, right behind the McDonald's and the bank.

It was almost sunset, not quite dark, when we pulled up to a duplex. A guy was flagging us down from the front yard. "He's upstairs, beating on her," he said frantically.

"Do you live downstairs?" I asked.

"No," he said. "I'm the boyfriend."

Wait. What? "If you're the boyfriend, who's beating her?"

"Her baby's dad."

Oh, man. The first thing that ran through my mind was, *Then what the fuck are you doing down here?* The guy just didn't want to get involved.

The stairs were steep, and as I approached the door I heard a *tink, tink, tink, tink,* like an aluminum bat rapping on a pipe. Gun drawn, I crept toward the apartment. There was a hole in the door where a circular deadbolt should have been, through which I saw a lady on her knees, her face covered in blood. The sound I was hearing was a metal pole connecting with her skull. I didn't even have time to absorb the horror of it; all at once I decided to kick the door open, and if that motherfucker made any move other than dropping the pipe, I'd level him.

The landing was extremely narrow, so I planted my left leg two steps down and kicked the door open with my right. That meant I was pointing my gun slightly upward as I shouted "Minneapolis police! Drop it!" As the door swung open, I saw the lady's one-year-old son standing between me and the perp, directly in my line of fire. Thankfully, the guy dropped the pipe right away, so any instincts I'd had to shoot him—some combination of reflex, adrenaline, and inexperience, which could have ended terribly—were negated. The kid standing just where he was gave me enough pause for things to settle down.

I thought we'd done our job. I'd stopped the beating, subdued the father without incident, and passed the lady off to paramedics. While I was assisting her, some late-arriving officers brought the guy to my car, which is an important detail when it comes to what happened next.

We drove to the jailhouse, and I passed the guy off to two detention deputies in the sally port before going inside to fill out paperwork. As they were booking him, those deputies found a gross misdemeanor's worth of marijuana—more than 42.5 grams—in his pockets. They came to me, incredulous. "You didn't see that?" one of them asked.

Scott looked shocked. "Didn't you check his pockets before you put him in the car?" he asked.

Fuck. I didn't even put him in the car, and I never thought to follow up.

Department policy held that if jail staff finds something, they have the responsibility of writing the report—and those guys didn't want to write the report. I had to go back out and charge the guy, then tackle the paperwork myself. As a trainee, I'd made a clear mistake. Sure enough, at the end of the shift Scott called out my oversight.

"You forgot to search for the marijuana," he said. "You should get a one on the five scale when I grade that. But I'm not going to give you a one."

"Why not?" I asked.

"Because you handled a domestic situation where this guy was trying to kill a woman," he said. "You were ready to shoot him, but instead you got him cuffed up, unharmed. You passed him off to other officers. You got the victim to safety and secured her medical attention. Nobody else did any of that. During all that time, somebody other than you should have been checking that prisoner's pockets."

They could have heard my sigh of relief on the Southside.

Then Scott added one more thing. "From now on, don't you ever put somebody in a car or bring them to the sally port until you've checked them thoroughly," he said. Message received.

Over the years, I've identified a lot of issues with the Minneapolis Police Department, both in how we relate to the public and how we relate to each other. My fifth FTO phase encapsulates a lot of them, for good and for bad. Mostly for bad.

The fifth phase is your final stop prior to becoming an official officer, and it takes place at what will become your permanent precinct. I was sent to the Fifth, in southwest Minneapolis, a wealthy neighborhood filled with lakes around which the city's fanciest homes have been built. The Fifth shares a border with the Fourth, but there is a world of difference between them. I'd have rather stayed close to home, but the Fifth was run by Kris Arneson, an ex-partner of my dad, who is so close to my family that she serves as my sister's godmother. Kris requested my assignment, and that made me feel good.

To that point I'd had a mixture of FTOs, some of whom were average and some of whom were really good. This FTO was neither. It is difficult for me to explain my feelings about him.

The night we met, I was amazed by his work ethic, or at least his rendition of it. He told me that a night earlier he'd made ten arrests. Ten! That's an amazing pace. Shit, I thought, this guy is some kind of supercop. That was okay by me. The more policing we did, the more I would learn and the more bad guys we'd get off the street.

Trouble was, we didn't get ten bad guys off the street. We didn't get *any* bad guys off the street. This FTO's "arrests" were actually misdemeanor citations, and I quickly came to learn his singular method for racking up such outrageous totals: looking for cars with malfunctioning license plate lights. All shift, every shift. In Minnesota that's a misdemeanor, and it's apparently what he based his record on. I kept asking for us to take calls so that I might experience different situations—as a recruit car, that was one of our mandates—but we rarely did. Traffic stops of a singular variety were our clear priority.

Fifth Precinct headquarters is on the far east side of the region, bordering I-35. Unlike most of the area, that neighborhood is home to a large minority population, primarily African Americans and Somali immigrants. Farther west gets you to the Uptown area with the lakes and big houses. I got an indication of this FTO's focus when I was behind the wheel on one of our early patrols and turned the car uptown. "Nope, we don't go that way," he corrected me. "We don't mess with taxpayers." Whoa. My first thought was to wonder why we were messing with *anyone*. For him, it was all about taillight tickets, and he sure didn't want to piss off wealthy Minnesotans with such tactics. Still, that's what he wanted, so that's what we did, in minority neighborhoods. I had to go along with it if I didn't want to get written up.

Well, I got written up anyway. The FTO docked me for damn near everything I did, no matter how small the infraction. Each evaluation was miserable. It's not like he tried to pinpoint something and then help me improve it. His criticism was always for different, nitpicky things, like not parallel parking on a high-priority call. (When my dad heard about that one he went up the wall.) When I performed well, it was dismissed. Once, a suspect ditched a gun out his window during a high-speed freeway chase, and a call went out to locate it. Among several cars searching, I was the one who spotted it. That earned a "Great job, Charles!" from the sergeant when we returned to the precinct, to which my FTO offered a dead-eyed response: "Well, he didn't find it. It was out there in the open, and he just saw it." Shit, seeing it had been our entire assignment. Nothing I did was good enough.

This act got old very quickly, but I was determined to buckle down, take orders, and endure. It was my last month of training, and I'd be an actual cop soon enough.

That's not how things shook out. At the end of the month, the FTO reported that I was not responding to his instruction, and thus not ready to advance out of my final training period. So instead of graduating with the rest of my class, I had to repeat the month. And instead of repeating it with a different officer as mandated by department policy, I was somehow assigned to repeat it with this same FTO. He failed me again, and I repeated it with him again. And again. And again. In all, I spent five months in the Fifth with the same guy. That's not how things are supposed to work.

I was so traumatized that I even took to calling in sick on occasion when I couldn't stomach the thought of driving around with this FTO all night. We both lived in the same Minneapolis suburb, and things got so bad that when I got off the freeway I would purposely go a block out of my way so I wouldn't have to pass his house and see his car in the driveway. That's how much I hated him. I was on the verge of quitting.

Everything came to a head during a nighttime traffic stop during that fifth month. The FTO was driving, which made it my job to shine our spotlight in the rearview mirror of the car we'd pulled over, a standard safety measure to prevent the driver from seeing what we were doing behind him. Even though it's typically the responsibility of the officer behind the wheel to approach the vehicle, he instructed me to handle the interaction. I did, and I found that the driver's license had been suspended. I wrote him up accordingly.

When I returned to the squad car, I said, "That was a good one. We got him."

The FTO offered no comment about how I'd handled the situation. Instead, he said this: "Where was your spotlight?"

I was confused. "I pointed it at his mirror, just like I'm supposed to," I said.

"It's not there anymore," he said. It turned out that as I exited our car, I jostled the spotlight just enough to shift it slightly. It was still pointing inside the car in front of us but was slightly off of the mirror. "That's an officer safety issue," he said.

I had conducted a drama-free interaction with the driver, discovered his suspended license, and given him a ticket. The car had just pulled away, and *this* is what the FTO wanted to talk about? I'd been with the guy for the better part of five months, and he'd flunked me four times for a laundry list of inconsequential reasons. That was all I could take.

"Man, I'm tired of your nitpicking," I shouted. "Everything I do is fucking wrong with you. You haven't taught me anything other than how to give Black people tickets for plate lights. You don't teach me *shit*." He shot back, justifying how those traffic stops were a valid part of police work. He said I was terrible when it came to officer safety. Then he stopped. We both did.

We drove in silence back to the precinct. He was going to make sure I felt this one.

Upon arrival, the FTO instructed me to wait in the report room, the place where I'd logged every broken taillight we flagged over the previous months. I sat surrounded by computers and forms while he went to see the shift sergeant.

After maybe twenty minutes, I was called into the sergeant's office. The FTO was there, too. "I've been told you were insubordinate and are not responding to training," the sergeant said. "I have called the inspector and the lieutenant, and we will set up a meeting tomorrow with the chief. Somebody will call you later with the details."

Shit. That's when I realized the fallout might be a bit more serious than I'd expected. It sounded like I could lose my job the next morning. I'd already been extended five times; maybe that was the point.

When I got home, I told my wife about the impending meeting but downplayed its importance. "It's just a review," I said. "Nothing big." I didn't want to upset her until I knew for sure what was going on. Inside, though, I was roiling. I barely slept that night, spending long hours in bed trying to figure out what to do with my life if policing was taken away.

I arrived at city hall at 9 a.m. and reported to Chief McManus's office. The receptionist buzzed me in with instructions that the chief would be along shortly. It was the same office where I'd held my advancement ceremony a few months earlier, a sizeable space with a couch, tables, and the chief's large wooden desk. I was the only one there, and I sat in one of the chairs facing the desk. On the opposite wall was the door to a meeting room. I figured that's where everybody was. The first to enter was the lieutenant, followed closely by the FTO sergeant.

"We spoke to your FTO," the lieutenant told me. "He reported that you were insubordinate and disrespectful. He says that you can't cut it as a police officer, and that you are not responding to training. You will meet with the chief, after which we will let you go. Your time with the Minneapolis Police Department is over."

Somehow, my entire career had been determined by one guy's negative opinion of me. What about the other four FTOs who gave me great marks? Did they not count? I was angry and afraid of what life might look like next. All I'd wanted was a fair shot, and I hadn't gotten it. The reality of the moment was catching up to me.

The lieutenant and sergeant returned to the conference room, and a few minutes later Chief McManus emerged. When he sat at his desk, the window behind him placed him almost in silhouette. He was new to the job, and though I'd met him briefly on several occasions, if he knew anything about me, it was sure to be that Charlie Adams was my dad. Everybody in the department seemed to know my father. In this case, Dad was part of the group that recruited McManus to Minneapolis in the first place, even in the face of a staunch faction of cops who were resistant to an outsider taking over. Dad had been a supporter from the beginning.

"Charlie Jr., they told me you had an altercation with your FTO," he said. He seemed almost confused. "They also told me that you haven't been responding to critiques, and that you have some officer safety issues. They say you're not able to succeed here, and theirs are the opinions that matter. Out of respect to you and your father, I'm here to tell you outright that we're going to fire you. Also out of respect for your father, I'm going to review the paperwork and explain to you in detail why things are happening the way they are."

At that point I could no longer hold my emotions in check. I sat in that chair and began to bawl. I had a young son at home and a baby in intensive care. I'd done everything in my power to support my family, and I failed. I failed them, and I failed my dad. I didn't know what else to do. The only thing I *could* do in that moment was cry.

That must have been tough on Chief McManus. He was a good man. Even though he'd been on the job only a short while, he'd established a solid relationship with our community and with my dad. I think he really wanted me to succeed.

Things grew strange as Chief McManus reviewed my Recruit Officer Performance Evaluation—the forms that the FTO used to justify drumming me off the force. I still had tears in my eyes as he made his way through the folder, lingering over each page before flipping it over and moving on to the next. I studied his face, but it was impossible to know what he was thinking. He read those pages for what felt like forever.

When the chief turned the final sheet and closed the folder, he did not say a word to me. Instead, he picked up the phone. "Get in here, *now*," he barked. With that, the lieutenant and sergeant entered. They stood at attention to the right of the desk.

Before Chief McManus addressed them, he turned his eyes my way. "Charles, do you have a lawyer?" he asked. Now I was confused. "Why, Chief?" I asked.

With fury in his voice, McManus gave me an answer I never expected. "If I fire you because of what's in this folder, you will own this department," he said. The guy was downright seething. He turned toward the lieutenant. Man, was I happy to not be on the receiving end of whatever he was about to say.

"Why the fuck was he with the same FTO for five months?" the chief spat.

Bingo.

"Reading these notes, every night it's something different," he said to the lieutenant. "Didn't anybody in this precinct consider that maybe these two just don't get along, and that Charles needs a change of scenery instead of being with the same FTO for five months straight? No recruit in the history of this department has been stuck with the same FTO for five months straight!"

Oh yeah, I thought to myself. *He's saying the good stuff now.*

The lieutenant stood stone-faced. I thought I spotted nervousness in her eyes.

Then the chief did something that awes me to this day. Anger rising, he addressed the lieutenant and sergeant together. "I want you to find me a Black officer for Adams to ride with, who will mentor him and show him the *right* way," he said. "And it better be one fucking great officer." The chief could easily have demanded that I merely get a competent trainer, not specifically a Black one, but he recognized that I'd worked exclusively with white people to that point and was aware of the barriers that could prevent me from getting a fair shake. He wanted to place me with somebody who had the best chance of understanding who I was and where I came from. He also wanted to remove any risk of race determining my outcome. A competent white FTO probably would have been fine, but if anything went wrong, there was always the chance that overtones of racism could arise. Pairing me with a Black cop eliminated that possibility.

Handing the task of finding an officer I could ride with to my FTO sergeant didn't make a ton of sense to me, given that he was the one who'd kept me with that other FTO to begin with, but I wasn't about to complain.

I was told to go home and wait for their call, and the three of us were dismissed. It took a few days, but they finally placed me. That's how I ended up with Tim.

Given the lack of diversity in the MPD ranks, one Black officer stood out as a perfect potential FTO. Tim Hanks was six feet tall and 220 pounds, a linebacker in a cop's uniform. He had a take-no-shit reputation, which was fine by me. Tim had been our range instructor, so I knew what kind of personality I'd be getting. There was a wrinkle, though. While most FTOs were regular patrol officers, Tim was part of a SWAT specialty unit called STOP—Strategic Tactical Operations and Procedures—a tactical task force aimed at gang and drug busts. They specialized in warrant services, not 911 response calls, and had no interest in pulling over citizens for broken taillights. That was also fine by me. My dad had trained Tim, so everybody figured I'd be treated fairly. I was transferred to his unit and told to start straightaway.

Tim was a badass cop. (These days, "badass" isn't always intended as a compliment when it comes to police officers, but Tim was a badass in all the best ways.) There was also no mistaking that he was *not* a field training officer. To say that he was reluctant to work with me is a wild understatement. Tim had read all the recent reports on me and was not impressed. He told me as much the day we met in the SWAT garage. "I don't want to do this shit," he barked. "It puts me in a bad position." Tim had heard the rumors flying around the department about me being a screwed-up trainee who didn't know what he was doing and didn't want to be in the position of deciding whether I was cut out to be a cop. He had a relationship with my dad and my uncle and didn't want that responsibility. In fact, the first thing Tim ever said to me was a warning: "Watch your step. I've heard a *lot* about how fucked up you are."

Damn, brother pulls no punches.

I spent my first couple of days on the job getting familiar with Tim's routine. Everything was proactive with the SWAT unit, which mostly did things like serve warrants and assist on calls. We were based downtown but did most of our work on the Northside, in the Fourth. Not only was that my home territory, it's where Uncle Tony was stationed. Tim made a point of making sure our paths crossed as often as possible.

During our second day together, Tim pulled me aside. "Hey dude," he said, "do you have a lawyer?"

Why do people keep asking me that?

"Every negative comment on your reports—and there are a lot of them—is not what I'm seeing in that car with you," he told me. "Really, the only negative observation I have is that you're not proactive enough with your traffic stops . . . and then I realized that's all that other FTO does, and you're probably tired of that scene. From where I sit, you're a damn good cop."

That gave me a lot of confidence. I finally knew that I was being evaluated on my total performance. It allowed me to stop trying to avoid mistakes rather than expand my knowledge. I finally got out of the dreaded "prevent defense" mindset. Tim even told me that I could parallel park the fuck out of a car.

Tim and I spent the next three weeks together, and I learned so much it was crazy. He taught me how to be proactive beyond traffic stops, surveying an entire neighborhood while on patrol. We kept our eyes open for cars on the hot sheet, suspicious activity in certain areas, and generally being aware of our surroundings at all times. He showed me how to clear loiterers out of drug-dealing areas, first by issuing warnings to move along, and then by taking IDs and making searches if people were still there the next time we came around. It's a tactic that helps keep riffraff away from public places and allows businesses to remain accessible, rather than having potential customers scared away by gang members congregated outside. I never did that in the Fifth Precinct with my previous FTO, but with Tim it became a staple of my patrol work.

One day, the hot sheet of stolen cars included a silver Chevy Malibu with gold rims that some gangbangers had been seen in. I was driving our regular patrol just north of Lowry Avenue when I spotted the car headed in the opposite direction. "There it goes!" I shouted. The street was narrow, and I had to make a three-point turn to swing the squad car around. They saw me a mile away, and turned onto a side street long before I could catch up. By the time I reached the intersection, they had turned again and were out of sight. They got away.

Tim was so pissed that he almost punched a hole in the dashboard. He literally dented the car. I didn't know if he was upset by my pursuit or disappointed they got away, and I wasn't about to ask. Our next few hours of patrol passed mostly in silence.

That night, Tim didn't even fill out my evaluation form. He was too angry. Luckily for me, his wife was also a cop, and she gave him some perspective when they discussed the situation later that night. He relayed their conversation to me the next day.

"I was really upset that the car got away, but Laura pointed out that you found the car in the first place, and I should give you credit for that," he said. "She was right. We'd all been looking for it, and you were the one who found it. You're gonna be all right." After an evening spent questioning my own abilities, that was good to hear.

Not long thereafter, Tim and I were assisting on somebody else's traffic stop. I recognized one of the guys in the car from a photo in our intel briefing. He was a known gang member and was wanted on probable cause, which was enough for me to get everybody out of the car and onto the sidewalk. When I flipped up the back-seat cushion, I found a veritable arsenal—a shotgun, a couple of handguns, and a semiautomatic. That bust was a breakthrough for me. It gave me so much confidence, especially after my previous FTO experience had broken me down.

Tim was tough on me like a big brother would be, and because it came from a genuine desire to help me grow, it was easy to take. I'd like to think Tim did it because he liked me, but he was a good enough cop to have done it for anyone. As it turned out, Chief McManus also had a vested interest in how I was doing. I saw this firsthand when, in the process of making a routine traffic stop, I put out a standard call for backup. Next thing I heard over the radio was "Car 1, I'll roll by." Holy shit, Car 1 is the chief! That's when I knew beyond doubt he was 100 percent down for me to succeed. The chief doesn't do a roll-by for anybody, but there he was, making sure that everything was right. When he arrived, he gave me a friendly nod. "You good, Charlie?" he asked.

Yes, sir. I'm freaking great.

One month with Tim rebuilt everything my experience with the other FTO had broken. The end of our time together was my ten-day audit, the solo stint that was the only thing standing between me and becoming a full-fledged policeman. I served it with Tim, who stayed entirely in the background, observing. My ten-day was flawless. On the eleventh day, I officially became a member of the Minneapolis Police Department.

Finally, I was a cop.

Chapter 4

Rookie to Resource

M y very first call of my very first day on the job brought me
to my old neighborhood at Twenty-Second and Irving,
less than a block from where I grew up. I was on solo patrol,
responding to a report of a citizen down. I pulled up to find
a thin woman in her late thirties sitting on the front steps of
a house. She was a mess, bleeding from abrasions across her
face and body, the consequence, I learned from eyewitnesses,
of being tossed from a moving car. She was too dazed to offer
much information, possibly due to her trauma but more likely
because she was drunk or high. She'd managed to crawl her
way up from the street, and the homeowner on whose steps
she'd chosen to perch wanted nothing to do with her. Or with
me. The only thing he wanted was for us to get off his property. Now.

Wow, I thought, it says something about a neighborhood
when a guy is more interested in getting the police out of his

front yard than in helping a fellow citizen. A lot had changed since I'd moved away.

I helped the lady to a nearby lot with some space for her to sit down. She was sedate until paramedics arrived, at which point she lost her damn mind. She'd been lying on the ground, and the moment they mentioned strapping her to the gurney (standard procedure for an ambulance ride), she began to punch and kick for all she was worth. That lady was in no shape to depart on her own, so the paramedics grabbed one arm each, and I moved to pin her legs. Before I even reached her, she kicked out and buckled my right knee. I landed in a heap on top of her. With that, the lady hit me with everything she could, scratching me something fierce. With me atop her, though, it looked to the crowd like *I* was trying to beat *her* up. They started yelling at me to leave the poor woman alone. Dealing with an addled citizen was one thing, but an angry mob presented a different level of concern. I pushed the "officer needs help" button on my radio.

Within what seemed like seconds, two squad cars pulled up, and the officers controlled the crowd while I focused on getting the lady into the ambulance. When it was over, my uniform was dirty and disheveled. I was a mess. I never did learn why the lady had been thrown onto the street.

As soon as I returned to my car, my old FTO, Tim Hanks, called.

"Man, how the hell you gonna have an 'officer needs help' call on your first day?" he laughed. "This is your *first* call on your *first* day!"

He was joking, but he wasn't wrong. Luckily it got easier.

The following week I was transferred to a permanent assignment in the Second Precinct, in northeast Minneapolis. That's where the University of Minnesota is located, across the Mississippi River from where I grew up. I was given the dog watch shift, from 9 p.m. to 7 a.m., which was fine by me.

It's not like any of Minneapolis's five precincts are more or less desirable when it comes to patrolling. A cop's satisfaction with his precinct mostly hinges on how busy he wants to be. The Northside, the Fourth Precinct, has the most serious crimes like shootings and robberies. The Southside, the Third Precinct, is nearly as busy. That's where the George Floyd situation went down, which I'll get into later. The Fifth Precinct, in southwest Minneapolis, was quiet enough for my FTO to spend most of his time running taillights. Then there's the First Precinct, downtown, comprising the heart of the city's nightlife.

For me, the Second Precinct was a godsend. I did not want to be at the Fifth with my FTO from hell, and I was not yet ready to deal with everybody I grew up with in the Fourth. The Second was the best of both worlds—not as busy as the Northside, yet still lively, with campus life stirring up some ruckus on weekends. We helped the university police with things like drunken frat boys, but the residential patrol stayed pretty quiet. Our biggest headache was a nightclub called Gabby's, which hosted hip-hop nights on Thursdays and Saturdays. Tons of people from the Northside would drive across the Broadway Avenue Bridge to attend and then hang out afterward at a nearby twenty-four-hour gas station, SuperAmerica. Fights sprang up in that parking

lot all night long. One Thursday a guy got stabbed. The following Thursday a guy got shot. The Thursday after that somebody
had his finger bitten off. We found the fingertip in the station's
convenience store, where the biter spat it out. Things got so bad
that management started closing the station between 1 a.m. and
4 a.m., until Gabby's owner, after ongoing legal tussles with the
city, finally sold the club.

My years in the Second were great, mostly because that's
where I met my partner, Todd Kurth, a light-skinned Black
man, short and kind of stubby, who became like a brother to me.
Tim Hanks set us up. We were the 211 car, Kurth and Adams,
working the southeast together to stop home invasions, engage
in foot chases, catch child abusers, and track down assault suspects. Oh, could Todd talk some shit. Every shift was ten hours
of comedy for me. We sang songs together while we drove on
patrol. We were goofballs.

For me, Todd's personality can be summed up with a single
incident. He and I were in the locker room before a shift, getting
ready for our roll-call meeting. Todd was running late, having
stepped out of the shower with only a minute to spare. I took off
without him, and I was as surprised as anyone when he strolled
through the meeting room door in the nick of time, wearing
nothing but his bulletproof vest, boots, and a towel around
his waist. There were six cops in the room, and we all thought
the same thing: *What is wrong with this dude?* When the sergeant came in, he didn't miss a beat. He and Tim were both
ex-military, and the sergeant ordered Todd to the podium with
a curt, "Kurth, front and center!" When Todd approached, the

sergeant snatched his towel away. I'd assumed Todd was wearing underwear, but boy was I wrong. Todd didn't even flinch, just stood there proudly, his business hanging out in front of the world. Todd is not the slenderest of cops, but he's comfortable in his body. Every cop in that room began laughing so hard that somebody had to close the door before we disrupted the entire precinct. We were on the ground in tears, every one of us. Somebody could have fallen over with a coronary, and he wouldn't have received any help because the rest of us were laughing too hard to move. The sergeant eventually handed the towel back, and during the exchange it accidentally fell to the floor. At that point Todd made a show of bending over to pick it up. Those of us who'd made it back onto our chairs found ourselves right back on the floor. There weren't any women in the room, so at least he had that going for him.

That was one side of Todd. The other was the police side, which he handled as well as anybody on the force. For me, the story that exemplifies our partnership took place on a weekend night after the bars closed, maybe 3 a.m. It was dead air in the Second, nothing going on. We had just returned to the precinct to do some paperwork when we received a call of two people fighting in the street. College campuses see a ton of fights every weekend, almost all of which end quickly, before the police arrive. So we let it go. A few minutes later, the call came up again: two people fighting. That was odd, but not so odd we felt the need to investigate. When it came in a third time, Todd and I headed to our car. Maybe there was something to it after all.

As we turned onto the street, sure enough there were two people down the block, brawling on the sidewalk. When we got closer, though, we saw that it was a woman and a man. He was on top of her, and her clothes were off. This wasn't a fight, it was a rape. I jumped out of the car and kicked the guy off of her. We cuffed him up and called an ambulance, but this story sticks with me because of what the woman said next.

"I was praying," she told us. "I said, 'Lord, please don't let him kill me. Lord, please help me.'" Then she said, "As soon as I thought, 'Lord, please help me,' the man disappeared."

That was the moment my boot connected with his head.

That really sat me down. I couldn't stop thinking that this lady's prayers to be saved actually *were* answered. Were me and Todd angels sent by the Lord? She'd prayed for somebody, and we arrived. At that moment the mundane hours required for police work faded away. This was why I joined the force—the chance to do something good for somebody.

Whenever Todd tells that story, he starts to cry. Already bonded, we were tighter than ever after that.

There weren't many Black cops in Minneapolis when I joined the force. Of the few who were there, most were older, like my dad and my uncle, and had been around for a long time.

A 2022 US Department of Justice research bulletin found that in 2020, about 12 percent of police officers nationwide were Black, about the same percentage as the overall population. In Minneapolis, 18.4 percent of the population is Black, yet African Americans compose only 9 percent of the police force. My class of twenty-something recruits included two. I was one of them.

There were some clear-cut rednecks in my precinct, but most of the racism I encountered within the department was focused on the citizenry, not on me or my fellow cops. The same cannot be said for my father. By the time I left the force in 2020, Dad had been a police officer for more than thirty years, leading the department's violent crimes and procedural justice divisions before taking over the Fourth Precinct. Dad had grown up on those streets, and his genuine connection with residents helped make him a great cop. I took that influence to heart. I also took his treatment within the department as a warning sign about what kinds of forces might be aligned against me.

The internal affairs crackdowns Dad faced as a younger officer—the ones that cost his partner and several other Black officers their jobs—were only the beginning. In 2007, when Dad was a sergeant with twenty-two years' experience, he was demoted from homicide detective into investigations—a move the department called a transfer, even though there was no mistaking its purpose. Dad and his partner, Richard Zimmerman, had the highest clearance rate in all of homicide, over 90 percent, yet he went from handling murder cases to more mundane things like auto theft. Police chief Tim Dolan, on the job since McManus left to take over the San Antonio Police Department in 2006, pointed to perceived insubordination as the basis for the move, but that's not how any of us Black cops saw it. Dad became the latest of four Black officers, and the one with the highest profile, to have lost prominent positions over the previous ten months.

A local newspaper, *MinnPost*, referred to Dad as a "superstar cop," one of the city's best homicide detectives. "I've never been written up for insubordination in my life," he said at the time. One incident stood out as the likely driver for Chief Dolan's decision, and it had nothing to do with insubordination.

Earlier that year, a bicyclist had been beaten to death in South Minneapolis, which the suspect pinned on a marijuana deal gone wrong. Dad was smart enough not to take that statement at face value; there was no supporting evidence, and even if it was true it had no bearing on the severity of the crime. His trouble began when the lieutenant in charge of homicide openly discussed the drug-deal angle with the press, giving it credence. It was an exceedingly stupid decision and was traumatic for the victim's family. Dad later compared it to a rapist claiming his victim deserved it because of what she was wearing . . . and the police actually listening to him. Dad publicly apologized to the family, a decision that, in the eyes of Chief Dolan, ran contrary to departmental position. The lieutenant called my father in for a meeting about it, and their exchange is what led to Chief Dolan's claims of insubordination. Well, Dad did curse during that meeting—once— and immediately apologized for it. We know this because the lieutenant recorded the conversation, without Dad's consent and against departmental policy, and the tape backs up my father's story. It didn't matter. He was branded and demoted anyway.

Dad was one of five Black officers—all with at least eighteen years' experience, all sergeants or lieutenants—to sue the MPD in 2007 for being bypassed when it came to promotions and overtime pay, and for becoming outsized targets for departmental discipline. Part of it had to do with his transfer out of homicide, even as his white partner, who'd made similar statements about the case, stayed put. Part of it had to do with Chief Dolan publicly referring to the decision as disciplinary action. To this day, Dad believes race was a motivating factor.

The suit also alleged a racially hostile work environment, including a hate letter sent through interoffice mail to every Black city cop back in 1992, which threatened each officer's life and was signed "KKK." Things improved when Chief McManus came aboard. He named two Black deputy chiefs, one of whom was subsequently demoted after Dolan took over. According to the suit, Dolan fired, demoted, or transferred every Black officer above the rank of captain, with the exception of one who'd already announced her retirement, leaving MPD with an all-white police command working daytime shifts.

Also according to the suit, the chief replaced the Black inspector of the Fourth Precinct with a white acting inspector who'd been the subject of multiple civil rights complaints, not to mention one of the largest police brutality settlements in Minneapolis history. That's who he chose to run the Fourth, the Blackest precinct in the city.

Other details in the lawsuit included a lieutenant, one of Dolan's "cronies," wearing a jacket with a "White Power" badge (the product of membership in an off-duty officers' motorcycle club with demonstrably racist membership), and allegations that as a teenager, Dolan himself had placed hate literature in the school lockers of Black students at North and Henry High Schools. The suit also claimed discriminatory hiring bias based on the department's former screening psychologist, who allegedly rejected a higher percentage of Black candidates than white. When that psychologist left the department, his replacement, tabbed by Dolan, made outspoken discriminatory statements about the LGBTQ community. Another part of Dad's suit had to do with a previous lawsuit, from 2003, which alleged a culture of racism within the MPD. In the aftermath, Minneapolis agreed to develop and maintain a strategy for improving diversity in recruitment and retention of officers, but when Dad filed his suit more than three years later, the department had finalized neither recruitment strategy nor a career-path report, as promised. The arrangement also included implementing a formal succession plan for supervisory positions and ranks, with a particular eye toward minority groups and females. No action was taken on that, either, or on the department's commitment to implement a mentorship program.

I was actually named in the lawsuit, not as a plaintiff but as an example of racism within the MPD. I'd applied to join the department's field training officer school in 2007. Having had my own miserable FTO experience, I figured that more quality trainers would help develop more quality recruits. They turned me down. The sergeant in charge pinned it on my performance as a rookie then changed his reasoning to the fact that I was too new to the force, even though I'd already been on the street for three years by that point. Later, we learned that white officers with less time than me had been admitted. (I ended up training officers anyway on a volunteer basis when the FTO program was shorthanded, though I never held an official title. The difference lay in the way recruits were channeled; because I wasn't part of the official assignment system, there was never an expectation that minority recruits would end up with me.)

The suit also named my uncle Tony, who'd applied to be an MPD cadre officer in charge of that year's recruits. The job went to a white woman with less seniority and fewer qualifications. The thread between my being turned down for the FTO job and Tony's being turned down for the cadre officer job is that both positions would have had positive impacts on minority recruitment—something about which the department appeared to care little.

Did Dad's lawsuit have any effect? Well, he settled with the department and got a bunch of money. More importantly, one of the other officers involved, Medaria Arradondo, became the city's first Black police chief a few years later. He served for five years, retiring in 2022.

There's one more way things have changed. In early 2021, Dad was tabbed to be the inspector of the Fourth Precinct, in the process becoming the first-ever Northsider to run that department. He made it a goal to work with the community instead of against it, and it is paying off. Who knows, with enough success, the rest of the department might even follow his lead.

I'm known mostly for two things: policing and coaching. Those worlds intersected early in my career, thanks to the Police Activities League. I started working with PAL before I was even a full-time cop, back when I was still a community service officer and attending school. The Police Activities League is designed to foster positive relationships between law enforcement and community youth, and I volunteered to chaperone field trips and transport kids to golf lessons. I also coached PAL-sponsored basketball and football teams in local rec leagues, arranging shifts so that I didn't start work until after practice. I ended up coaching with PAL for seven or eight years, then returned in 2015 (by which point my uncle Tony was running the program) to coach my son, Adrian.

The next step in my coaching evolution came via working off-duty security at North High football games. That's how I got to know the head coaches, Tony Patterson and Rick Williams. I asked if they needed any help; they did, and in 2007 I took over North's ninth-grade team and became offensive line coach for the varsity. By my third year I'd moved up to varsity defensive coordinator, during which time our squad's record went from

2–7 to 9–3, and we reached the state tournament for the first time in nearly a decade.

Making the journey extra special was that during that time a job opened up within the police department's juvenile division for a school resource officer. SROs are basically cops whose beat is a local campus. It was perfect for me. I'd already been working off-duty security at North, not only at sporting events and dances, but in the hallways during school hours, assisting the full-time MPD officer assigned there, Henry Scurry. The available SRO job wasn't at North High, but Henry agreed to transfer to a different school so I might take over at my alma mater. Just like that, I was back in the Fourth Precinct.

Some SROs wore their full uniform to work, but I opted for lower-key khakis and a polo with an MPD patch. I kept my gun out of view in a small holster beneath my shirt. (I drew it on a number of occasions over my years at North, but never inside the school.) At North High, most of the threats to students come from outside our perimeter. The most dangerous time of day is when school lets out, at which point people can swoop into the neighborhood and wreak havoc as kids head home. In gang territory like ours, that threat is real. I devoted significant energy to preventing people from loitering on our block, and making sure that people who didn't attend North were nowhere nearby when that dismissal bell rang.

Students took to calling me OA, for Officer Adams, a name they use to this day. I stayed in that role for thirteen years. The way I saw it, SROs were on campus less to enforce discipline—

that was the administration's job—than to serve as a liaison between the community and the police department. I was an in-house resource, able to handle warrants without a 911 response. Parents and kids came to me about issues, some of which had nothing to do with school, because they knew I would treat them respectfully. More times than I can count, somebody wanted to pass along a tip about some goings-on in the neighborhood, but didn't want to risk being spotted entering a police station. Coming to talk to me raised no flags; they were just going into the high school. I could do all that policing—filing reports, writing out tickets—from my office at North.

My holistic approach took some time to develop. I received an early lesson back when I was a part-timer, working security at North in addition to my regular patrol. Support staff was struggling to contain a kid following a classroom fight, and they called me to assist. I arrived to find two deans, the assistant principal, and a social worker already on the scene, and a teenager so large, so strong, and so out of control that I ended up cuffing him for the safety of those around him. We eventually sat him down in a counseling office while the administration contacted his mother. That's where he began talking big shit to me. "Fuck you, pig," he said. "Fuck all you cops. You're lucky I have handcuffs on because I'd beat your ass. I'd fuck you up." Typical stuff.

The guy was relentless, and eventually he got on my nerves. Finally I walked over and removed his handcuffs. "Okay," I said calmly. "Step on up." He'd challenged my manhood, and I was ready to hold him to his word. Thankfully, he knew better. "Man, I ain't about to fight no cop," he said. I gave him a long glare and sat back down.

To my benefit, Big Spank—Mike Favor, my first varsity coach at North—was by that point principal of the school. Mike set me straight, pulling me aside and telling me bluntly how inappropriate my reaction had been. "These are *kids*, man," he said. "You can't work in here the way you patrol the streets."

"Ah, well . . ." I stammered. "I . . . the thing is . . ."

I had no real answer because I knew Mike was right. For me, part of policing had always been staying in take-no-shit mode. On the streets, if I saw guys congregating at a known drug-dealing spot like the Wafana Market on Lyndale Avenue, I'd tell them to hit the block. That was my cue for them to clear out; if they were still there the next time I circled around, I took that as an invitation to intervene. I had no problem getting physical with a suspect.

That was the attitude I brought to school. I was the big, bad cop, and whatever I said was to be taken as law. I wasn't about to beat anybody up in the hallways of North High, but I had not yet defined the limits of my police tactics. That meeting with Mike helped me change course. He made it clear that I was not the face of rules enforcement at the school. That was *his* job. Mostly, he wanted me to watch the administration's backs while they dealt with whatever issues arose.

After that first confrontation, I realized I had to get better at de-escalation. No matter how much those boys might have resembled men, they were still just teenagers, and by their very nature teenagers tend to talk more than they should. I started walking the hallways with that old rhyme, "Sticks and stones may break my bones but words will never hurt me," running through my head. I even developed a motto: *As long as you're walking, I don't care about talking.* When the dismissal bell rang at the end of the day, it was my job to clear kids from the campus. ("Hit the block and keep it moving" quickly returned to my vocabulary.) I received some pushback, frequently in the kind of salty language that until very recently would have set me off. Now, though, a random "fuck you" didn't bother me a bit, as long as whoever said it was headed someplace else. If they were walking, I didn't care about the talking.

I broke up a lot of fights through my years at North, but I didn't give out many assault citations. I came to view a scrap between two kids as mutual, although review of the security tape would occasionally show one student jumping another, and those kids would be charged. For serious incidents I might even arrest somebody, although they almost never saw the inside of a squad car. The vast majority received misdemeanor tab charges—a citation without a trip to jail—at which point a parent could pick them up or an administrator would take them home. For higher-level charges like first-degree assault, featuring serious injury or use of a deadly weapon, I would call for a unit to take the offender to the juvenile processing center. I'm proud that over my thirteen years as the full-time SRO at North, nobody was ever shot, stabbed, or killed.

I came to find that being from the neighborhood was a decided benefit to my line of work. One standout moment involved a meeting in the principal's office with the family of a student who had hauled off and hit me as I tried to restrain him following an altercation with one of his classmates. He was a smaller kid and the punch was superficial, but I charged him with fourth-degree assault—attacking a police officer—and disorderly conduct. His mother was irate at the charges, livid that I'd laid my hands on her son. She demanded consequences and threatened to sue the school. Thankfully, her father, the student's grandfather, was also in the meeting. He'd started off as angry as his daughter, but as soon as I walked into the room, the entire tenor changed.

"Hold on," the grandpa said, turning to the kid. "You got into it with Spank?"

I could only smile. I'd known this guy about my whole life. He was a long-standing member of the community.

"Me and Spank's granddaddy grew up together," the guy proclaimed. "I know his daddy. I know his uncle. I know *him*. No Adams is going to disrespect somebody unless they're being disrespected themselves. If you got into it with Spank, we don't play that."

Once that connection was made, not only did things settle down, they took a turn for the positive. "If you need anybody to have your back," the grandfather told the kid, pointing at me, "this is the man you turn to." From then on, I paid the boy some extra attention and made sure to check in on how he was doing.

He became a lot friendlier. When you work inside your community, that's how things go.

That kind of encounter was on the easier end of the SRO scale. The opposite side involved premeditated violence by students and a genuine lack of concern when it came to the welfare of their classmates. One time, a couple of girls from another high school came to North looking for one of our students. Our building is locked from the inside during school hours, but a friend opened a door for them, and they walked the halls until they found their victim, then beat her so badly she needed medical attention. A review of security camera footage showed us who let them in, and it didn't take much sleuthing to pinpoint the aggressors' identities and what school they attended. They were charged with trespassing and assault, and their accomplice from North was expelled.

Groups of girls getting into scraps was actually a bit of a theme during my time as SRO. Just days from the end of one school year, a bunch of girls jumped somebody from a rival group in an unused hallway. Unfortunately for everybody, they decided to broadcast the assault on Facebook Live. I was sitting at my post near the front door when two or three cars screeched up and a bunch of adults raced toward the building. When I asked what was going on, a woman shouted, "My daughter's being beat up *right now*." I was in the process of telling her she was mistaken when she pulled out her phone and showed me the live stream. Holy shit. I needed to take action, but letting those adults into the building would bring certain chaos. I held them at the perimeter and radioed for support staff to break up the fight. I wish things had ended there.

The adults at the door were extremely agitated, and being refused entry to the school set them off. Within minutes more people arrived, and then more. I don't know if kids inside were calling people or word got out about the live stream, but soon cars were piling up in the parking lot, with hordes of angry people storming toward the entrance. Everybody wanted in. They never made it, but a bunch of students—including all those girls, still actively brawling—worked their way into the parking lot. Before long, parents were fighting, too. It was pandemonium, a damn near riot. I initiated a schoolwide code red, telling teachers to keep their kids inside the classrooms, called for backup, and focused on making sure nobody had any weapons. I used my mace to drive people backward, toward the sidewalk. Get them moving, keep them moving is a mantra of crowd control. After a couple of squad cars arrived for support, we ended up issuing a bunch of citations for disorderly conduct and took four people to jail. We also shut down the school for the day and spent the last few days of the semester on code yellow. The kids involved in the fight weren't allowed back onto campus, which kind of didn't matter—those girls kept fighting on the streets and in public parks all through the summer. Based on the behavior of their parents, it's not hard to see where they got it.

That's as messy as things ever became for me, but dealing with angry parents wasn't so unusual. When they realized a cop was involved in disciplining their child, they'd come down and scream at me about putting their son in handcuffs or whatnot. I dealt with hundreds of situations in which parents were mad at *me* for their kid having gotten into trouble.

Maybe the worst was when North High was shot up. In the wake of one horrific school shooting after another in this country, this one barely registers, but for people on the scene—and especially for the guy in charge of security—it was really scary. Unlike more publicized incidents, this had nothing to do with an angry, disaffected youth taking out his rage on fellow students. This one was all about the fucked-up nature of violence in our neighborhood. It was 2019, and I was in my office—acting not as an SRO but as the school's football coach. I was in the middle of a recruitment meeting with the coach from the University of Northern Iowa about a couple of Polars, including my son, Adrian. In the middle of our conversation I received a notification on my phone from the MPD's ShotSpotter system—a device that audibly detects gunshots and can pinpoint where they came from. My alert read, "Four shots at 1500 James." Oh my God. *That's our school.*

I ran into the hallway to find people racing back and forth. The top window of the outside door had been shot out, and bullets littered the hallway. Kriss Burrell, a dean at the school and the freshman football coach, was yelling at everybody to clear the hall, and we quickly locked everything down. When I went outside to assess the situation, nobody was there. MPD was shorthanded at the time and unable to respond, so I literally had to handle a school shooting scene by myself. At least no one was hurt.

When we reviewed the video, it showed somebody on the opposite corner, at Fifteenth and Irving, shooting at a student as he pulled into the parking lot—a response to some mess that had recently gone down in the streets. I found out later that this was actually the second time the kid had been shot at. Somehow, he and the people he was with all made it into the building safely.

On the video, the shooter, wearing a dark hoodie and dark pants, ran east on Fifteenth Avenue. That wouldn't have been enough information to catch the guy, but luckily for us, I was tipped off by a student to look at a social media post by somebody fitting that description, uploaded from just down Fifteenth Avenue shortly after the shooting. In the video, the guy said he knew where the victim's cousin lived and threatened to shoot that place up, too. That was all we needed. We found him the next day, still wearing the same hoodie.

Some people decry the presence of SROs in public schools, but I can say with confidence that no outside officer responding to that 911 call would have had the same leeway as me to investigate the episode, let alone cultivate the kind of inside-the-school sources I had. Chalk one up for the good guys.

Chapter 5

Mountain Climbing

In 2009, I was in my third season as assistant football coach when North High finally made it over .500, going 9–3 to reach the state tournament. Hopes were high for the following year, until we nearly went under.

Not the football team. The entire school.

Almost two years earlier, in 2008, a charter school opened only a half-mile from North. We began to lose kids, slowly at first, then in a deluge. The process seemed to feed on itself, one North High family after another transferring their kids out, some to the charter, many others to suburban schools outside the district. By the time the school year started in 2010, a school built to hold 1,700 kids, which only six years earlier boasted an enrollment of 1,100, was down to 265 students, only 40 of them incoming freshmen. On the first day of classes, 52 kids showed up. Those hallways were *empty*. Reducing our presence to a single wing of classrooms barely masked the desolation. Some days we damn near had more staff than kids. It was heartbreaking, especially for those of us who had grown up there. You could feel the end coming. Things grew so dire that in October, just after football season began, our superintendent proposed shutting the place down entirely. It was no small idea: North High School had been serving Minneapolis since 1888.

It all prompted one question: What the hell happened?

It's impossible to lead with anything besides the fact that the neighborhood no longer looked like it once did. North High had been founded as an entirely white school, but a hundred years later, in the 1980s, nearly half the student body was Black. By 2022, the number of Black students was up to 90 percent and less than 3 percent white. It was more than color, though—it was economics. In 2022, almost 70 percent of students at North High qualified for free or reduced-price lunch, and the Northside had the highest rate of housing foreclosures in all of Minneapolis.

Beyond demographics, or maybe because of them, it seemed like the district had set up North Community High School for failure. They'd closed a spate of elementary and middle schools over recent years, a number of which, like Lincoln, Willard, and Franklin, were feeders for North. This was especially impor- tant given that North was the only high school in Minneapolis without an attendance zone, meaning it was the default high school for exactly nobody. Kids who lived a block away could be assigned to rival schools like Henry or Edison. Whatever the district's vision, propping up the disadvantaged residents of the Northside did not seem to play a part.

The kids weren't the only ones to flee. So did the principal and many teachers, who took jobs at other schools or found new professions entirely. The entire football coaching staff packed up and moved to Robbinsdale Cooper High School in the nearby suburb of New Hope. Coaches do that kind of thing when they think their school is about to shut down. That's how I came to take over the program as head coach in 2010. I was just as worried as the departing coaches, of course, but as a North High alum and Northside product, I was deeply invested in the success of my school. When I accepted the job, I wasn't sure there would even be a program to take over.

Luckily, civic outcry spurred the district to hold off their plans to shutter the place. North High parents, alumni, and community leaders flooded school board meetings, voicing opposition to closure. To give us a lifeline, the district superintendent set an enrollment threshold for North's 2011 freshman class . . . which we didn't come close to reaching. Somehow, the superintendent let that go, too.

Instead, she hired a consultant out of New York whose specialty was reviving schools. Just like that, our suddenly small institution became classified as an arts and communication academy, with a separate academy focusing on science, technology, engineering, and math. As I understand it, those decisions helped justify the low enrollment, since only a limited number of people were accepted. The transition to arts wasn't much of a stretch; North already had a history as a magnet school and housed the radio station for the entire district—KBEM, jazz radio. (I was a DJ there back in the day. "This is Charles Adams, student at North High, and you're listening to John Coltrane on KBEM, 88.5 FM.") With the change, seventy-five minutes were added to the school day, which affected me mainly because it meant I couldn't start practice until 4:15 p.m.

My first season as head coach was rough. I didn't get the job until a week before camp opened, and I found a roster so sparse that I spent part of my regular weekend police patrol knocking on players' doors to inform them of my new position, and to urge them toward practice on Monday. That might have been a winning strategy in some neighborhoods, but when a police officer knocks on Northside doors, people tend not to answer. I must have hit a dozen houses and managed to connect with only five or six players.

I ended up with a sixteen-man roster that year—eleven players on the field and five on the sideline come game day. I don't know how, but we managed to win three of our nine games. It was like a season-long fire drill.

Little did I know.

After that 2010 season, the district leaned in to North High's academy transition and decided to fresh-start the school entirely, replacing virtually everybody from the principal on down. Even the boys' basketball coach, who'd just won the district's coach of the year award, was let go, so it shouldn't have been surprising when I was fired, too.

I guess I wasn't fired outright. Like every other coach I was given a chance to stay, but I had to reapply for my position and hope for the best. I wasn't having that. I was *already* the head coach. Ego got the better of me, fueled by the uncertainty of the process. If they decided to go in another direction, I'd be out of a gig, and it might be too late to find something else. Plus, I already had another job lined up. When word of the school's plan got out, the football coach at Park Center Senior High School, in the Minneapolis suburbs, asked me to be his defensive coordinator. His name was Rickey Foggie, and he'd been the starting quarterback for the University of Minnesota Golden Gophers for four years in the 1980s, where he played under legendary coach Lou Holtz. That sounded pretty good to me.

I'd already spent a couple of seasons coaching ninth grade basketball at Park Center, having been recruited by North's former coach when he moved over there, and I was familiar with the landscape. The place I really wanted to be, of course, was North High—it was my alma mater, and I was still the SRO there during working hours—but Park Center actively recruited me, not to mention it was a bigger school with a much higher profile. Also, there were no rumors about it being shut down.

I canvassed everybody I knew about whether I should take the job. They all said North was on its way out, and Park Center was a great program that could lead to big things. Everyone agreed. Everyone but my dad. "Absolutely not," he said when I asked his opinion. "Going to Park Center is a horrible idea. Stay at North."

Dad knew a little bit about Park Center because my little brother Styles had gone there to play football as a freshman before transferring to Champlin Park, just down the road from Dad's new house. Dad didn't care too much for Park Center's program, but mostly he was a North alumnus and knew how desperately the school needed quality leadership. He didn't say it outright, but I think that's really why he wanted me to stay.

I didn't listen. I took the job as defensive coordinator at Park Center.

At my first practice I mostly concerned myself with getting the lay of the land—meeting the kids and learning what kind of schemes the team ran. Their defensive backs coach had been around a while and had some firm opinions. That was fine with me, except that whenever I tried to say something to the team he jumped in and talked right over me. That's weird, I thought. I'm the defensive coordinator, and he's a position coach. This was not the kind of energy I wanted on display in front of the kids.

I like to be up front about things, so that night I gave the coach a call and asked outright if he had some issue with me that I should know about. Maybe he was upset that I'd gotten the job instead of him. "It seemed like you were brushing me off whenever I tried to speak," I told him. "I didn't want to say anything in front of the players, but I can't have you undermining me like that. I just want to make sure we're on the same page. Is there a problem that needs addressing?"

Nope, he said, he was just trying to coach those kids. He downplayed the interaction and told me that everything was good. It wasn't. I could tell from his tone of voice.

The following Monday I was scheduled to meet with the school's athletic director to finalize my contract. He called me just before I came in. "Hey, so I just talked to Rickey," he said. "He says he doesn't need you coaching for him anymore."

Excuse me? The guy had no further details. I was out of a job.

I called Rickey to find out what the hell was happening, and he didn't answer. I called him again throughout that day, and then throughout the week. He never picked up, and he never called me back. To this day I haven't spoken to him, and I still don't know the real story. Unfortunately for me, North had already hired a head coach by that point. It was football season, and for the first time in many years I would not be coaching football.

Luckily, the guys I'd worked under as an assistant at North, Rick Williams and Tony Patterson, brought me on as assistant offensive line coach at their new school, Robbinsdale Cooper. It was a volunteer role, but there's nothing sadder than a coach with no team. I was happy to take what I could get.

I was fortunate that the Polars' season opener fell on a Thursday, an off-day for Cooper. I provided off-duty security on the field and was shocked by what I saw. The team somehow had fewer players than our bare-bones roster a season earlier, and even fewer fans in attendance. The program was unorganized, with the new head coach constantly yelling not only at players but at his assistants. They literally screamed back and forth from press box to sideline disagreeing about plays. The kids themselves got into it, sniping at each other with increasing volume as the game progressed. I'd coached most of them a season earlier, and I wouldn't have tolerated any of it. Finally, I couldn't take any more. "Hey y'all, cut that shit out," I snapped at the bench. "Lock in and get into this game. You frustrated at each other? Take it out onto the field." That message should have come from the coaches, but hearing it from a nearby cop was better than nothing.

A bad scene didn't get much better. North lost to a bad South High School squad, 30–0.

After the next game—a 53–30 loss to an Edison team that would win only once more all year—parents circulated a petition to remove the head coach. Their frustration came partly from his lackluster system, and even more so from the way he treated his players. Morale had disappeared. Players were being punished during practice for routine mistakes that should have been utilized as learning experiences. He had his skill position players—not the big guys who relied on strength, but the little guys who relied on speed—push a car from the parking lot around the track in 95-degree weather without any explanation as to why they were doing it. Probably because there was no good explanation. Things got so bad that this coach lost his keys during the game at Edison and afterward made the entire team scour the field on hands and knees looking for them. As if that wasn't bad enough, there had been some recent shootings in the area, which, combined with bad blood between Edison players and North players, was enough for the coaching staff to plan a quick entry and exit, to minimize North's time in the neighborhood. Yet somehow there were the kids, crawling across the turf looking for lost keys. It simply wasn't safe.

My SRO office at North High was just down the hall from the principal and the athletic director, and at some point that week they began arguing so loudly I could hear them from my desk. I didn't think much of it—those kinds of arguments happened all the time—until I heard our AD say, "We should've kept him in the first place. We should never have let him go."

Hold on. What was she talking about?

A moment later, she was at my door. "Charles, I have a hypothetical question for you," she said. "If we had to get rid of our head football coach today, is there any way you would coach the team? If so, again hypothetically, how much time would you need to prepare?"

I didn't even pause to reflect. "Make an announcement to have every football player meet me in the auditorium at 3 p.m.," I said. Conversation over.

At 3 p.m. they announced my return as head coach. I'd been gone only about a month. Even though we lost every game the rest of that season—we could barely field a varsity roster—I could tell it was the start of something better.

I did a lot of learning that year. At first, I'd thought coaching was all about the plays you call and how well the team performs. With a squad like that, though, where any hope for lasting success was years away, I came to realize that my job actually hinged on the health of the program and its players. I learned that I needed people around me who bought into my vision, which allowed me to delegate responsibility and focus on the players instead of the plays. A big part of that outlook came from my father.

Dad had played collegiately and coached for years in the Police Activities League. Shortly after I was reinstated, I asked him to come by practice to help evaluate our secondary. He did, and he never left. He was working middle watch for the MPD at the time, and each day came to practice directly from roll call. (What police do on their time between calls is discretionary; Dad always kept his radio with him and took off whenever he was needed someplace else. It worked out pretty well for everybody.) My father is a good guy to work with. On the field he respects me as the head coach and has no problem telling people I'm the boss, if only to make sure there are no questions about it later.

When Dad arrived at that first practice, there weren't even ten players on the field. "Where is everybody?" he asked, shocked.

"This is it," I sighed.

The guy looked like he was about to cry. Back when he played, North had been a robust, vibrant high school. He couldn't believe how far it had fallen.

We didn't have much in the way of talent or experience on the roster, but kids started having fun and buying into the program. Instead of punishing them for things they did wrong on the field, I corrected them. There's a big difference. Some of the kids who'd quit actually came back. It began to look like a football team.

One thing giving me optimism was a bunch of exceptionally talented neighborhood eighth graders I wanted to recruit. They'd been playing together since they were little, and I wanted them *all* to be Polars. They had numerous options for where to attend high school, and I did my best to short-circuit that process. I had recently taken over as North High's co–athletic director (a position I held for a year until it became a full-time post and I would have had to give up coaching football to maintain it), and I made an extremely aggressive move: I offered their two primary rec league coaches the chance to take over our freshman team. They were quality coaches, so there was little downside to the move, but to me their greatest asset was the ability to convince the entire lot of players to join our program—especially the group's leader and quarterback, Tyler Johnson.

I cannot overstate how special this group of kids was or how instrumental Tyler became to our success. He'd been in line for a scholarship at a local high school football powerhouse, Academy of Holy Angels, and if he didn't come to North it seemed likely that his teammates wouldn't either. Tyler lived just a few blocks away from school, so while he awaited the Academy's decision, I invited him to work out with us, hoping his teammates would show up, too. He came, and they did.

I don't know the details, but that scholarship never materialized. Even then it was no sure thing that Tyler would choose North, which made me even happier when I hired Larry

McKenzie to coach our varsity basketball team. The move had nothing to do with Tyler—Larry had won four straight state titles with our rival, Patrick Henry High, and was one of the area's best coaches—but Tyler also played basketball, and I knew he wanted to play for Larry. That might have been the final factor in bringing him to North.

I've devoted so much space to these high school recruits because, in the end, they meant much more than athletic success to North High. Our school, the heart of our community, the thing we could point to as a symbol of our ability to rise above, was on the verge of collapse, and the void it threatened to leave was massive. The residents of Minneapolis's Northside carried that weight, and that fear.

Tyler and his cohort helped change all of that. When they joined the football team, the program came to life. We started to win games, and we became a beacon to others around the area, kids who otherwise would have explored other high school options. Something good was brewing on our campus, and the whole Northside could feel it. Our success built on itself, and with it an outpouring of support from area residents desperate for a symbol of positivity on which to focus. North High, once such an integral piece of our community, was returning to its former place of prominence, raising all those around it in the process.

How we got to that point is itself a good football story.

I'd initially figured that by the time those incoming freshmen were ready to jump to varsity a year or two down the road, our team might be pretty good. It took me until midway through our very first seven-on-seven summer scrimmage to ditch that plan completely. Tyler, Malik Matthews, and a bunch of other freshmen tore the field up that day. They just dominated the competition. We'd lost every game a year earlier, and many of our holdover seniors, whose attitudes weren't great to begin with, didn't even show up to play that day. The decision to start the freshmen became easy.

The group was approachable, confident but not cocky. They were tough. Most of all, they were determined to win. Even with that group, our team wasn't yet good, going 2–6 for the season, and in the section tournament we lost to Kerkhoven-Murdock-Sunburg 54–40. That playoff game was held deep in farm country, two-and-a-half hours outside of Minneapolis, at the kind of field that required people to park in a ring around the sidelines with their headlights on. The loss was dispiriting, but there were plenty of positives to take away. The Polars were down 35–0 at halftime, and then we clawed our way back to respectability, Tyler to Malik, one bomb at a time. The Polars owned that second half. Hardly any of our supporters made the trip, and when the game began, only a handful of people were sitting on the visitors' side of the bleachers. By the fourth quarter, though, our stands were full of folks who had been inspired to come over and cheer us on.

The comeback was nice, but that's not the part of the game that sticks with me. Just before halftime, a Kerkhoven player broke his femur while being tackled. It was a clean play, and there were no bad feelings on the field beyond concern for the kid. The game was delayed for a long time while medics did their jobs. As soon as I understood how serious the situation was, I led my players to midfield and we joined hands in prayer. I ended up with my arm around the player's mom while several North players helped the kid onto a stretcher and then into the ambulance.

We didn't think much about it, but it seems that Kerkhoven fans took note. As we walked to our bus after the game, folks from both sides of the bleachers gave us a rousing ovation. They even showed up with an unexpected stack of pizzas for us to eat on the ride home. We didn't really understand it at the time, but a few days later I received word that somebody in Kerkhoven's camp had written a note to the state high school league, saying they'd never seen a team show such care for an opposing player. The injured player's mom sent us pictures of us praying for her son. The local paper ran photos of us consoling the kid on the field. I had our entire team sign a North High T-shirt and sent it to the player.

It had been a rough season for my freshmen, but they were learning. Not only that, they were inspiring others to do the same. A bunch of kids who lived close to North High, who'd chosen to go to other schools to play football, transferred back home. Our roster jumped from nineteen players to fifty, and the next year we went 6–2, especially impressive considering we'd won a total of five games the previous three seasons combined. Our guys were improving by the week. Tyler was becoming a star. We were on our way.

One measuring stick was Kerkhoven-Murdock-Sunburg, the team we'd lost to in the section playoffs a year earlier. This time around we kicked their asses. What a difference a year makes. The kid with the leg fracture was still out of action, but he was really excited to see us. He gave me a big hug as I walked onto the field.

Everything came together the following season, 2014. We went undefeated, outscoring our opponents 327–24, including four shutouts. Then we rolled through three straight wins in the section playoffs to qualify for North's first state tournament since 2010. In my experience, any successful program requires leadership from players as well as coaches. Every great team I've been part of has had at least one kid who demands unquestioned respect from his peers. He doesn't have to be the best player, or even a star, but luckily for me Tyler checked all those boxes. During his time at North, I didn't have to do much to get my guys into line. Tyler did it for me. He'd tell players to lock in and get their shit together. He told them to be quiet when they were disruptive, to be on time if they were late. Literally, the guy would wait at the gate and get on the ass of whoever straggled in after they were supposed to. That was leadership right there.

And it wasn't just Tyler. There was Isaiah Matthews, a big offensive lineman who we called Pookie. Pookie and Tyler were best friends and were on equal footing as team leaders. Linebackers Kori Randle and Dallas Griffin were also looked up to by everybody. Those guys were like coaches on the field. (Occasionally, Tyler *was* a coach on the field. Late in some blowout games, he'd grab a play sheet, put on a headset, and run our offense for a while.)

That was Tyler's junior season. His biggest play came in our state tournament opener against Blooming Prairie. Just before halftime we faced third down on our own nine-yard line. I called a designed run for Tyler, who raced ninety-one yards for a touchdown. Five yards from scoring, he somehow fumbled the ball. Nobody was within fifteen yards of him; he just straight-up dropped it. Somehow, it bounced directly back into his arms. Tyler danced into the end zone without breaking stride.

As we walked to the locker room at halftime, a black SUV pulled up. Four coaches from the University of Iowa piled out and offered Tyler a scholarship on the spot. Talk about drawing focus from the game plan. During the second half, Tyler was clearly distracted. On defense he missed assignments left and right, and I could hardly blame him. I can only imagine the whorl of feelings inside his head. We barely held on to win, 14–6, giving me my first state tournament victory as a coach.

What truly made the day consequential for me—far more than Tyler's epic run or our advancement to the next round—was that my grandmother, Shirley Adams, my dad's mom, had passed away that morning. I called her Gramps. She'd been ailing for some time, so it wasn't much of a surprise, but this wasn't easy for me or my dad. He texted me with the news while I was on my way to school that morning, and I turned around to meet him at the nursing home. Uncle Tony was there, too. So was Kris Arneson, Dad's good friend from the MPD.

Before we parted ways, Dad and I talked about the most appropriate way to approach that night's game. As head coach,

I felt a strong responsibility to be there, but it would be easy enough for Dad to take the night off. The playoffs are important, but not *that* important.

He wouldn't hear of it. "Gramps was a football fan," he said. "There is no way she would want either of us to miss this game." At that moment I was particularly happy to have Dad on my coaching staff.

We were able to put aside our grief for a few hours, at least until the end of the fourth quarter. It was cold outside but not windy, and on fourth and goal, Blooming Prairie had an opportunity to take the lead. Just as their quarterback lofted a pass toward the end zone, a gust of wind—the first of the day—pushed the ball off course and into the arms of our defensive back, Keyon Thomas. That's when I knew Gramps was there with us.

When the final whistle blew, my dad and I found each other at midfield. "This is for Gramps," I choked. We broke down in each other's arms, crying big tears as players milled around us. We'd never had a moment like that together.

Our season ended the following week with a loss to Dawson-Boyd, in a game that would have sent us to the state championship. Our team was talented, but as a coach I fell short in one key area: focus. By that, I mean we'd been so bad so recently that all season long my target had been simply reaching the state tournament. Once we made it, all of us—myself included—acted surprised. We'd reached our goal and were at somewhat of a loss about what to do next. After that game, I vowed that I would never let that kind of thing happen again. I never did. The outcome in 2014 was disappointing, but we were buoyed by the fact that Tyler and his cohort were only juniors.

The next year, 2015, is where it all came together. We went undefeated for the second straight season, outscoring our opponents 276–20. You might have noticed that's a lot fewer points than a season earlier, and there's a good reason for that: two of our opponents were so reluctant to play us that they forfeited instead of taking the field, for which we were credited with two points of offense per forfeit. Both claimed they weren't healthy enough to play, but I had my doubts. I had to schedule a last-minute scrimmage in Wisconsin just to keep our guys sharp. (We were up 32–8 at halftime in that one when our opponents decided they didn't want any more, so that game ended early, too. It was a long drive for two quarters of football.)

That season Tyler went nuts on the field, completing more than 60 percent of his passes for 1,557 yards (222 per game) and twenty-one touchdowns. He intercepted more balls as a defensive back than he threw as a quarterback—that's a straight-up video game statistic—and ran two of them back for touchdowns. He also rushed for more than six hundred yards and nine TDs.

We won our two games in the section tournament by gaudy scores and rolled through our first two opponents in the state tournament, putting up fifty-four points and sixty-one points respectively. With that, the Polars were in the state championship for the first time ever. Our opponent in Prep Bowl XXXIV was Minneota, a high school from a small, football-crazed town of the same name about three hours west of Minneapolis—a perennial power and the defending Class A state champs.

In the week leading up to the biggest game of our lives, my team found itself hamstrung in the face of a nasty stretch of winter weather that barely allowed us to practice. Snow forced us into the North High gym, where we were limited to low-level walk-throughs—hardly the type of preparation a championship game required. When I think about it now, it's clear we should have rented out a domed field someplace, but I'd never been in that situation, and the idea didn't occur to me until later. (We learned our lesson the following year, when we rented the covered field at Concordia University for a day, then practiced at Holy Angels' covered facility, which they let us use free of charge.) The championship game was outdoors at the University of Minnesota's football stadium, which boasted a heated field to prevent snow from accumulating on the turf.

Minneota had been dominant all season, a detail about which I didn't care. All I wanted heading into that game was to make sure my kids were right, and fully prepared to carry out their assignments. To us, Minneota was just another good team. That was the only way to view it without getting caught up in overanalysis.

The plan worked, at least early on. The Polars led 12–7 after the first quarter (thanks in part to a thirty-four-yard touchdown pass by Tyler and a sixty-four-yard touchdown run, also by Tyler), and we trailed only 20–18 going into the fourth.

From that point on, though, it was all Minneota. We'd game-
planned thoroughly for their lead running back and had done
a formidable job against him, but the kid tore his ACL playing
defense in the first quarter. At that point we figured we had
things locked up. Then their backup RB—the injured player's
younger brother—absolutely killed us, rushing for 108 yards and
three touchdowns. It was more than enough. We lost 35–18 as
Minneota rolled to its second straight state championship. It
was Tyler's final game as a high school player.

Afterward, a lot of attention was devoted to a play that happened with about five minutes remaining and North trailing by
nine: One of our players was caught on camera poking an opponent in the eye while he was on the ground. I was somehow
perceived to be laughing when I saw it, which, come on, not only
do I not condone that type of behavior, but how the heck could
I have even seen something like that from the sideline? I didn't
even know it had happened until somebody told me about it
afterward. It was all over the news, even getting some national
run. Suddenly, instead of our great second-place finish in the
state, we heard mostly about how dirty the Polars were.

I received a lot of hate mail about that. The incident made
me look bad, but more important it made the team look bad. It
was a stupid thing for our guy to do, and it hardly represented
our program. I couldn't discipline him because he was a senior,
and that game was his last for North High, but the school suspended him for the first two wrestling matches of the upcoming season. I thought that was the end of it until we heard that
Minneota's coach and athletic director wanted the kid to travel

out to their campus and deliver a handwritten apology. By that point I'd had enough. My player had done something reprehensible, for which he was punished by the school. We're talking about a seventeen-year-old with a lot of growing up to do. He sure as hell would own the consequences of his actions, but I wasn't about to make him drive hours into the sticks to read out some apology. At that point it seemed mostly like they wanted to humiliate him. Hell no, we're not doing that.

Football teams must walk a fine line. We're at our best when we have some fierce players I can let loose. I train my guys to level opposing ball carriers in legal but unforgiving ways. This is how football games are won. To maximize ability, you must push right up to the edge of being penalized. I have made my boys acutely aware of what kind of plays I will tolerate and what kind I will not. Even though they sometimes cross that line, they still have to respect it. Always respect the line.

We'd have all off-season to consider that notion.

I find winning football games to be extremely gratifying. Preparation teaches kids discipline, teamwork, and the ability to take instruction. Success lends pride to the school and the neighborhoods that surround it. Over the years, however, I've learned that wins and losses are not the only way—or even the best way—to measure success.

Back when I was a coaching assistant, a senior on the team found himself on the street after his drug-addicted parents were evicted from their house. He was taken in by a family member who lived far from school, and I ended up picking him up and dropping him off every day on my way in and out. Later, I helped connect him with a college, Vermilion Community, just a few miles from the Canadian border. My sister Brittney was playing basketball there at the time, and I'd made some connections on the athletic staff. This kid encountered a few bumps along the way, but he eventually returned to Minneapolis and opened a successful barbershop. I bring him up for a couple of reasons, neither of which has to do with portraying myself as some sort of savior, which I most definitely am not. Mostly, this story shows what can happen when community members take a vested interest in their own. He may have made it without my help, but smoothing the road for the disadvantaged is the best thing we can do to help people rise above. And my neighborhood needs as much of that as we can get.

I've encountered many similar stories, with a wide variety of particulars. I remember a sophomore who wouldn't show up at his parents' house for days on end. His mom reached out to me over and over, telling me how he was running the streets and that she was worried sick. As the North High SRO, I knew that standard procedure dictates parents of runaways ultimately have to pay the fines of whatever citations their kids accrue. In this case, though, the student was coming to school every day—he just wasn't going home afterward. I tried to talk sense into him, but nothing worked. Finally I resorted to threats. "I'm going to call your mom each night," I told him, "and if I learn you haven't gone home, I won't let you into the school." Over the next two days that's exactly what happened: I called his mother, who told me she hadn't seen him, and when he arrived at North I sent him away.

On the third day he showed up with a proposition. "OA, I'm safe," he insisted. "I spend nights at a friend's house. Please let me come to school. I *have* to come to school, I have to get my work done."

It was clear that he wasn't telling me the whole story, but the kid was earnest. I met him halfway, telling him that as long as he was safe and his mom knew where he was each night, I would work with him. The offer came with a caveat, though. "One more thing," I told him. "As of this moment you're on the football team. You'd better be at practice tomorrow, and every day after that." He agreed.

Not long thereafter I heard from an administrator at the local middle school the kid's younger sister attended. She was having issues of her own, he said, and he wanted to prep me because she was slated to attend North High the following year. He told me their mother had a serious drug problem and a boy-friend who didn't seem to care too much for the children. My new player had avoided mentioning those details to me.

It's amazing how quickly you can identify your blind spots once they're pointed out to you. I saw all at once that I had placed far too much emphasis on the mother's story, and not nearly enough on the son's. For a guy whose jobs—both as SRO and football coach—hinged on listening to kids, I was shocked by how poorly I'd listened to this boy. The question was right there for me to ask: Why was he coming to school but not going home? There *had* to be something more to the story, but when he was reluctant to talk, I never dug deeper.

The next day, I called the kid in for a meeting and heard his story with different ears. This time I knew where to prod, and sure enough he opened up. He was able to say that he loved his mom, even as he acknowledged her failures, and he told me that his stepdad was her supplier. He was clear about wanting to avoid trouble for them—it's why he hadn't spoken up earlier— which was fine by me. My focus was on him, not them.

I saw football as an opportunity for that kid to gain something he was missing at home: a team atmosphere, support, camaraderie. It was also an opportunity for me not only to watch over him, but hopefully inspire further trust. He came to practice every day, even amid the chaos at home. He was only an average player, but he enjoyed interacting with his teammates, and I was delighted to have him around.

You might ask: What made me think the kid could be a football player? The answer is easy: nothing. It didn't matter. You don't have to be a football player to play football. You *become* a football player once you start playing. It's my job to teach the sport. If you can run, catch, or tackle, I will find a place for you. And if you're on the team because it benefits you more than it does me, that's fine, too. I am convinced that the structure and discipline that boy found on the football field helped him through to graduation.

I'll offer one more story here about taking care of people, and it's not about one of my players. It's about a security monitor at

North High named Kelly Woods, who started working for the
school before I came onto the scene. Kelly was from the streets
and had done time for things like drug trafficking and auto
theft. Then he changed his life around. He became the school's
protector, always looking out for me and the students. Kelly was
very loyal, a great guy.

Kelly garnered public attention in 2007, in an unfortunate
way. It happened just after a talent show at the North High
auditorium. As people filtered out of the building, two groups
that had already left the show began shooting at each other.
Everybody else raced back into the building, jostling to get
through the doors. Thankfully, nobody was hit. I was inside and
radioed for support, but when investigators came to the scene
they found no shells. We later learned that was because Kelly
had raced out to cool things down, and not only had he pocketed
the shells, but he grabbed the gun that fired them and stashed
it inside his wife's purse. Why would he do that? The shooters,
members of a local gang, were North High students. Kelly knew
them, and he did what he thought was the right thing: once the
danger had passed, he tried to protect them. He took their gun
and told them to get lost.

Let me be clear: it was a stupid thing to do. Abetting criminals and hindering a police investigation in order to protect
gangbangers were about the worst decisions Kelly could have
made in that moment. Had I been out there with him, it never
would have happened. Regardless, it's easy to see the purity of
his motivation.

Kelly's involvement came to light just an hour or two later at a nearby gas station, after he got into a top-volume argument with an ex-girlfriend that had nothing to do with the incident. By that point, the gun Kelly had confiscated was in the back seat of his car. Witnesses saw it, the police were called, and Kelly was arrested. He faced a third-strike charge as a felon in possession.

Soon, a petition in support of Kelly circulated through the school in hopes that he might avoid jail time. I received a subpoena from the prosecutor to act as a character witness *against* Kelly, so I called her up and told her I thought that was a bad idea. Kelly and I had a good relationship, and I was among those who thought he shouldn't be locked up. The prosecutor saw my reluctance to testify as dereliction of police duty and raised a fuss. In the end, none of it mattered. I took the stand and said nothing but good things about Kelly, and he went to prison anyway.

These stories illustrate just how close to the edge so many people in my neighborhood are, even many of the good ones, and how just a little bit of support along their journey might lead to better outcomes. How developing relationships rather than dealing with trouble as it arises can deeply affect long-term results. The more involved I got with the kids at North, the more I wanted to be involved. I felt blessed that my job allowed me to be on campus every day, keeping close tabs on those who needed it.

Summer vacation turned out to be a different story. SROs typically spend their summers reverting to more typical policing, patrol work and the like, until school returns to session. That was a long time for me to be away. After connecting with kids and their families all year long, helping divert them from trouble, I didn't want to encounter those same kids in my squad car come July and August. At least I wasn't primarily assigned to dispatch; instead of taking 911 calls, I'd usually go to the spots where kids hung out and try to make connections. It wasn't much, but it was something.

Those summers are the main reason I developed the Minneapolis Police Department's Brain and Body program in 2011. The Police Activities League was already hosting weekly trips to a water park throughout the summer, which seemed like a good place to start. My own kids were at home without much going on, and I began to picture a program that might suit their needs during the summer months. Four or five days per week filled with sports activities and field trips could keep them occupied through the entire vacation. SROs could run it, and we could recruit kids from local high schools to help out.

Brain and Body was an immediate hit. Through PAL, we took kids ages seven to eighteen swimming and golfing; played every sport we could think of; and went on field trips to state parks, science museums, Twins games, and the zoo. It was all free. Many Northside kids had never experienced summer camp before Brain and Body, and they ate it up. To this day my children talk about it as one of their favorite experiences ever. The friends they made there are still with them, which is exactly what camp is supposed to do. Most of my job with the MPD was geared toward keeping people safe, but with Brain and Body I got to substantially improve kids' lives. Over two decades with the force, coming up with that program is my proudest achievement. To me, it shows what police departments can do when they truly have the best interests of the community in mind. I only wish that was a standard instead of an outlier.

Chapter 6

Rebuild, Rebound

It's the middle of the 2016 football season. The Polars are getting manhandled by a pretty good team from a much bigger school. We're down five points going into halftime, and I want to keep my guys engaged. As the players jog off the field, I pull my dad aside. "Once everybody gets into the locker room, gather the team up," I tell him. "Make sure to put the water bottle carrier in the middle of the floor. I'm gonna storm in and kick the hell out of it. Then I'm gonna yell some, I'm gonna glare some, I'm gonna turn around, and I'm gonna storm out. Once I'm gone, I want you to say to the team, 'Man, I've never seen him this angry.'"

Now *that's* a good football play.

It's also an exception. My strength as a coach isn't putting on inspiring performances for my players. It's not even X's and O's. I mean, I'm a pretty good play-caller, but there are probably coaches within my own division who can out-scheme me. What

I am good at—*really* good at—is reaching my players, grabbing on, and making sure they recognize the proper path in front of them, even if they choose to ignore it. Put that in place and the football piece almost takes care of itself. It took me some time to realize this.

When I started out as a high school coach, I ruled with an iron fist. Everybody was intimidated by me. Now, more than a decade in, that shit no longer works. Kids aren't necessarily different than they were back then, but their circumstances sure are. When I played football at North in the 1990s, we were student-athletes. We did our homework (Lord help us if we didn't—thanks, Dad), and if we worked part-time jobs, it was strictly on the weekends. My obligations were going to school, playing football, and, importantly, being a kid. I could focus on one thing at a time because my family didn't rely on me for necessities. I never had to help pay the bills, and neither did most of my friends. These days, too many of my players are the man of the house, and much of their time is spent filling in for somebody who left responsibilities on the table. They have to work or the rent won't get paid. They provide transportation for their younger siblings. When I was in high school my biggest chore in addition to picking up my sister and brother from Mom's was babysitting Brittney, and even then I'd just bring her to practice and let her run around on the sideline.

I have to keep all of that in mind when I lay out expectations for my players each year. If somebody can't get to practice because he is responsible for childcare in his family—"Practice starts at 4, but my mom doesn't get off work until 6, and I have to pick up my little brother at the bus stop at 3:45"—I accommodate however I can. Bring the kid to practice. He can sit with me while you get your reps in. I'll toss a football with him, let him run the bleachers, jump in the sand pit, drive me around in the golf cart. You being at practice is the most important thing; if you're here, I'll figure out how to make the rest of it work. Whatever it is, we do all we can to make sure football does not come at the expense of family responsibilities.

I've even had players—and cheerleaders and team managers—bring misbehaving siblings to me looking for some semblance of discipline. You're acting out at school? You don't want to listen to your teacher? Okay, you're going to start running, and I'm going to watch you do it while your sibling practices. After that, they tend not to act up anymore. That kind of thing happens more frequently than one might think.

If it seems like a tall order to look after a bunch of kids while I'm supposed to be engaged with my football team, it is. And that's just fine. I have capable assistant coaches for just that reason. They can handle the details of practice. Even without sideline distractions I tend to move around, watching sessions from every angle. Then, when the team meets in the middle of the field to close things out, it's up to me to break everyone down . . . and maybe kick some water bottles.

When I address the team, I think back to my great-grandfather, Daddy Jewel, the greatest deacon in all of Minneapolis. As I've explained, that man was able to fill a room with his presence, commanding the pulpit with power, filled by the Holy Ghost. Daddy Jewel believed what he was saying, so we all believed it, too. I try to emulate that as a coach—not from a religious aspect, but in fully embracing whatever message I deliver.

As I've mentioned, when Daddy Jewel spoke to the congregation, it felt like he was talking directly to you. I think about that often. When I speak, it's not only to the players, but to the coaches and even the community at large. I want to reach anybody with ears. That's how Daddy Jewel prayed.

Early on, I was overly concerned with being the best, trying to climb the ladder from assistant to coordinator to head coach, and during that process I lost my focus on the players. My goal was to be in charge, and it took some time to recognize what that actually meant. It's easy to get so wrapped up in day-to-day planning that you lose sight of the program. Coaches are in a position to touch everybody involved with their teams, and are frequently too myopic to even realize it. Go on, coaches: listen to the kids on the sideline. Listen to your assistants. Listen to the crowd. Be available. Be vulnerable. For me, that is all connected to how my great-grandfather led his church. It's about the people who trust you, and who you trust in turn. It's recognition that the people you work for and the people you work with are one and the same.

I was stubborn when I first took over as head coach at North. It was my way or nothing. I left no space for other ideas. I mean, it's still my way, but these days I solicit as many ideas as I can from as many people as possible. There's power in community. When North finally reached the state championship game in 2015, it was a seminal experience, and losing to Minneota was humbling. It made me realize that while Tyler was an undeniable blessing to our program, his presence also came with a downside. He was a wonderful young man, a world-class athlete, and a natural leader—so special that I came to rely on him too much. My primary strategy had been "We have Tyler Johnson, and that's all we need." Tyler was the greatest player to ever grace one of my rosters, but we needed plenty more than one great player to win. I haven't made that mistake—about Tyler or anybody else—since.

That championship loss taught me that I had to maximize everybody's performance. Not everybody gets to play wherever they want to, of course, but these days my practice players are just as important to me as the stars. If you're sitting on the bench, I want to make sure that you're the best bench player you can be. That can mean many things: supporting your teammates, being ready to enter the game at any time, buying into the team culture however you can. One of my current goals is making sure everybody gets to play at least some of the time. I don't consider race, physical ability, mental acuteness, grade level, or even gender. A number of young ladies have played for the Polars, and not just as kickers. Tori was a linebacker, and Sakari played on the offensive and defensive lines. Those girls were *strong*. My special teams coach, Beulah Lee Verdell (everybody calls her Miss Beulah), has been with the program since the 1990s, before I was even a student at North. They are all part of my holistic approach: to succeed, I need everybody invested. That's when the positive results come.

I had bits and pieces of all that before 2015, but it was only after losing to Minneota that I put the entire outlook into place. I sort of had to. We lost eleven starters from that roster, including Tyler, who went across town to the University of Minnesota. It was addition by subtraction. Before, opponents just had to focus on stopping Tyler. Now they had to stop everybody. My job was to make sure everybody, whoever they were, was prepared. The next year, 2016, that was our focus.

We won the whole damn thing.

My biggest wins as a coach come when kids with narrow prospects, or even significant impediments, succeed beyond expectations. This happens frequently, but the kid I think of first in that regard is the linebacker who, at four years old, was trapped in a Northside house fire and ended up with third-degree burns across most of his body. His face was ravaged, he lost four fingers on his left hand, and he was absolutely covered with scar tissue. The boy was in a coma for a month and given only a 20 percent chance to survive. He was still having reconstructive surgeries by the time he reached high school, and nobody took him for a football player. Not until he came out for practice, anyway, and I put him on the team.

His name is Taquarius Wair. Everybody called him TQ, and he became one of our best defensive players, going on to play college ball at a local JC. In 2020, he won ESPN's Jimmy V Award for Perseverance, and the network made a short documentary about him.

TQ was a neighborhood kid, with older brothers who went to North. I watched him grow up and knew all about his attraction to football. To that point in TQ's life, people around him tended to focus on his disabilities, but that part didn't matter to me. It's my policy to welcome anybody willing to accept what I'm trying to build, and Taquarius wanted in. He joined the team and stuck with it, in the process developing the kind of confidence necessary to bring other players along on his ride. By his senior season, TQ was a key voice on our sideline, effectively becoming a player-coach. I loved him for that.

Taquarius succeeded in part because he was naturally talented, but I've had plenty of average athletes who ended up playing at the next level, even becoming All-Americans, because they trusted me to put them in a position to succeed. One kid, Davon Townley, didn't even play football until his junior year. His mom wanted him to focus on basketball, and I tried to convince him otherwise. "Just give me a try," I told Davon. "If you don't like how I do things, you can always leave." The kid is six-foot-six and 270 pounds, and ended up getting a full scholarship to Penn State. He'll probably go to the NFL.

In my neighborhood, occupying kids' time with athletics is a great way to keep them off the streets. Once football season ends, those who don't move on to other sports frequently have little to do. Those are the guys I try to stay engaged with year-round. How are you doing? What are you doing? How are your grades? Let's grab something to eat. I have a burgers-for-A's policy: taking kids out to eat when they do well in school. I'll even occasionally boost it to J's for A's when somebody from the community is willing to finance some Air Jordans.

Those are great strategies for building productive citizens, but they don't always work. I haven't fielded outright gang-bangers on my North High teams, but in our neighborhood it's impossible to go too far before you encounter somebody with affiliations. Maybe it's a friend, a cousin, or even a brother. Kids get sucked into things in unexpected ways. Being a police officer allowed me to dig deep on this topic. My players know I will never condone criminal activity or ill-intentioned behavior, but they also know that if they end up on the wrong side of the law, I have their best interests at heart and will always treat them fairly.

Gangs dominate our neighborhood. They're called the Highs and the Lows, based on the street numbers of their territory— north of Broadway are the Highs, and south are the Lows. The neighborhood I grew up in is Highs territory, though back then gang life in my neighborhood involved the Vice Lords, the Gangster Disciples, and the Crips, some of which had national reach. Today's gangs have their own thing going on. The corner of Broadway and Lyndale is a huge place for dope dealing. The Winner Gas Station at 626 West Broadway is known as the Murder Stop because of all the gang activity there. Beef between the Highs and the Lows is the source of most of our shootings, and North High is basically on the border between them. Some real street dudes have been on my teams, guys who, while not actual gang members, are all about that life. There haven't been many, but they tend to make an impression.

When I think about that stuff, I think of Jamin.

Jamin Smith was a kid from the streets who always seemed to find trouble. Gang life is pretty much all he knew. He'd been raised in it. Jamin came to us in 2016 from the Hennepin County Home School, a juvenile correction facility that sent him our way partly because of our program's well-defined structure, and partly because Jamin's uncle had played for me, and his family knew about my reputation as a police officer and coach. Jamin is far from the only kid the system has tossed our way, and I've tried to embrace them all. Everybody deserves a chance. I think it's important for young people to learn from their mistakes and achieve positive goals, not to mention have fun playing football in the process.

For Jamin to even appear at our preseason equipment hand-out, he had to be accompanied by his probation officer. That arrangement lasted until he was fitted for a house-arrest ankle bracelet, which gave him the freedom to attend school on his own. When Jamin first arrived at North he was out of control, constantly cussing everybody out during practice. No coaches wanted to deal with him. He almost got to throwing blows with our own quarterback *in the middle of a game*. He was bitter and dismissive, and when we couldn't get him to fully participate in practices and drills, he didn't play.

Somewhere along the way, one of my assistant coaches noticed a Facebook post Jamin had written, saying that while football was his thing, he wasn't getting his opportunity at North and would probably head back to the streets. When my dad heard about that, he knew just how to translate it. "OA, we have to go a bit easier on the kid," he said to me that day at practice. "Let's free him up and see what happens."

So Dad sat down with Jamin. "I know you want to play, but you're not showing us anything in practice, and your attitude is horrible," he told him. This is where a career's worth of police work came in handy. "Jamin, think about it," Dad said. "When you were locked up in the County Home School, how many of your gang buddies put money on your books so you could buy some snacks?" Jamin couldn't name even one.

Dad continued. "So you're out there banging for these knuckleheads, and none of them will show up with a little bit of money for you?" he said. "I listened to jail calls all the time when I was in homicide, and every day I heard people begging for five dollars, begging for *two* dollars. 'Can't you *please* just put some money on my books?' These are gang members, grownups, and their buddies ain't coming to their aid. They were out there shooting people for the gang, and now nobody from the gang is looking out for them at all."

I don't know how deeply Jamin felt that conversation, but he sure enough came around. His attitude improved, he began taking instruction at practice, and he even made some friends on the team. By the end of the season he was one of our lead running backs. Jamin returned a kick eighty-one yards for a touchdown in our first section playoff game, and rushed for another score in the game after that. He ran for ninety-five yards and a score in our state tournament opener, scored another touchdown in our state semifinal win, and caught a touchdown in our championship victory over Rushford-Peterson. By the end of that streak, he'd seen enough positive reaction from teammates, coaches, and fans to do a complete one-eighty. He let us in, and we embraced him for it. Jamin had believed in his own ability from the start, and now everybody else was on that bandwagon with him. That's where the transformation happened, fed by the fact he now had people on the team—myself and my dad primary among them—who unequivocally cared about him as a person.

One thing I noticed about Jamin was that he never stopped worrying about what he'd do with himself once football season ended. That's when he ended up back in the one place he knew, hanging out with guys he shouldn't have been hanging out with. After our 2016 section championship in St. Cloud, our bus was driving down Broadway toward North High School. We passed a fast-food joint, and Jamin said, "Man, I can't even go there anymore—every time I'm near that place I get shot at." He wasn't joking, but he laughed when he said it. My dad overheard, and piped right up. "Boy, that's not funny," he snapped. "This is your life we're talking about."

"Ah, Sarge"—that's the players' nickname for Dad—"you always want to take it to another level," Jamin said. Shit, I only know one level when it comes to getting shot at.

A few weeks later, during our championship victory at U.S. Bank Stadium, Jamin made so many plays on both offense and defense that he was a regular on the big-screen replays. During one of those moments when he knew the camera was on him, that fool went and threw up a gang sign. Not many people watching knew what it was, but Dad and I sure did. At halftime, my dad got all over Jamin in the locker room. "That's not just an in-house feed—we're on TV!" he yelled. "I will slap the shit out of you if you do that again." Jamin was apologetic. I really don't think he understood the impact that kind of thing can have. Then again, the kid was irrepressible; he did it again in our post-game team photo. That was maddening to me, but it was tough to stay mad at Jamin. By and large, he was a model player and well behaved within the program.

Jamin's first real trouble as a Polar came at the end of his senior season. Players were supposed to clear out their lockers once the schedule wrapped in November, but Jamin ignored that instruction. A thousand warnings that items left in the facility would be set out for anybody to take had no effect. For Jamin, that included an expensive pair of Air Jordans. A kid on the baseball team ended up grabbing them, and when Jamin heard about it he was none too happy. He demanded them back, and the kid refused. "They were thrown out, and I got them," he said. "Now they're mine."

That's how the beef started.

By that point, Jamin had reconnected with some dudes from the street, and when he spotted this kid at the park over the weekend, he started talking to his friends about how he was gonna mess him up. Well, that's the kind of crew you don't make idle threats around, and Jamin ended up firing a couple of shots toward the kid and some North students he was with, including one of Jamin's football teammates. I like to think it was intentional that nobody was hit, but one of the bullets ricocheted into a squad car parked nearby. Everybody saw it happen. When the kid called the police to report the shooting, the officer he spoke with knew exactly where to turn. I got a call that afternoon.

"We're looking for your boy, Jamin," my colleague told me, and filled me in on the details. I was disappointed by the news, and I called my dad to talk it through. I also alerted the North administration that Jamin was wanted for second-degree assault, and that if he showed up for school I should be notified immediately.

I got to school at about 7:30 a.m. that Monday, a half hour before classes were to start, and found Jamin waiting for me in the computer lab by our weight room, hoodie up and head down. I was angry with him for fucking up so badly, and I was angry that he came to school and put me in a position where I was the one who had to take him to jail. Once we started talking, though, I realized it had to be this way. "OA, you're the only cop I know who will treat me fairly," he cried, tears streaming down his cheeks. I started crying, too. The boy was absolutely forlorn.

That was Jamin's senior year. Instead of going off to college, he went to jail. He didn't even get to walk with his class.

I was called as a character witness at his trial. Without condoning the violence or the crime, my father and I spoke truthfully about Jamin's character and the good we saw in him. I talked about his leadership on the football field, and how he and I were able to connect despite his troubles. Dad said, "I can't tell a young man I love him only when he's picking off passes and scoring touchdowns for me, then turn my back on him when he does wrong." We tried to get Jamin tried as a juvenile, and we even found a locked facility where he could continue his education and play football. The judge did not agree; Jamin was tried as an adult, and took a three-year deal that he served at the Minnesota Correctional Facility in St. Cloud.

While Jamin was locked up, one of his childhood friends was murdered on the streets, at a community kickball game. The game had ties to the North High football team, given that it was put on by Tyler Johnson's dad and one of my former coaches at North, Londell Anderson, and it took place at North Commons Park, kitty-corner from the high school. That kickball game was a huge affair, with cookouts and nearly four hundred people in attendance. A bunch of my former players were in the crowd, as well as many current players. One of the former players was Nate Hampton, who as far as I know was minding his own business when a guy walked up and shot him, right in front of everybody. Nate died on the spot.

There was no shortage of witnesses, but the shooting was gang-related, and people were too scared to come forward. Nate's presence lives on among the current Polars, many of whom knew him, because he was such a part of us. Every year at the anniversary of his shooting, some of our former players go to the park for a memorial. (The Polars actually practiced at that park until the shooting, but we changed spots shortly thereafter and haven't been back since. The threat of violence is simply too great.)

It was with Nate in mind that Jamin found his way back into trouble. On the day he was released from prison, he went to the site where Nate was gunned down to hold his own belated memorial. It probably would have been fine, except that Jamin's mother mentioned his plans on social media, inadvertently alerting everybody who might still have a beef with him to his whereabouts. Well, Jamin didn't arrive on time, but two of my other players, Pookie and Kori, did. So did Jamin's grandmother. They all got shot. Nobody was killed, but you better believe that stirred up some action on the Northside. Just a few minutes later, somebody went to 626 West Broadway, the Murder Stop, and lit it up. It was Jamin . . . or so they suspect. Thinking about what he might have done makes me physically ill, but his grandmother had just been shot, so it's not difficult to pinpoint his motivation. My dad was head of the MPD's homicide unit at the time, and he was on top of the entire incident. It didn't take long before Jamin was back in prison. As of this writing, he's still there.

Jamin's problem was typical of so many of my kids at North: after he finished with school he had nothing left beyond the gang environment he'd been raised in. It was his whole life. We thought we'd put a hook in him when we embraced him into our program. Jamin was very much part of our state championship. The kid's smart as heck and could have done whatever he set his mind to doing if only he could have gotten that gang stuff out of his system. Heartbreakingly, he didn't.

I failed him in that way, I think. Jamin knows that I care about him, but I didn't offer him anything to do or anywhere to go once football season ended. I keep thinking about the moments immediately following the final whistle of that championship game in 2016, when Jamin got hold of our trophy. He held that thing like a baby. The boy was genuinely thrilled. At that point I thought we had him.

Instead, he got lost, and he never gave anybody a chance to find him.

The Twin Cities District plays in Section 4 of the Minnesota State High School League, which comprises seven classes based on enrollment size. For most of my coaching career, North High played in Class A—the smallest division in the state, apart from seven-on-seven. We've improved attendance since the days when we barely had a hundred kids show up to school, but we're still at only about four hundred students. Being classified as a small school means I have to fill our nondistrict schedule with as many quality opponents as I can. That adds up to a number of road trips, frequently to small towns, hours away. Usually, this is fine. Sometimes, though, rural communities have a difficult time with a team that looks like ours.

In 2016, we played a preseason scrimmage about an hour southeast of Minneapolis, at Glencoe–Silver Lake High School. It was a unique format designed to maximize exposure to opponents, with four teams total, two at either end of the field, switching from offense to defense after ten plays apiece, then back again. After a half hour, you swap opponents. One of those teams was from New Prague, a small farming community whose student body is almost entirely white. We quickly learned that some racist motherfuckers live out there. New Prague fans had already been accused of making monkey sounds at basketball games and flashing white-power hand signals at hockey opponents. Think that mindset's not ingrained? Their students once wore KKK robes as part of a school play. Things were so bad that a couple of local districts decided not to compete against them at all.

Not us. We were fresh off losing the 2015 championship and had some chips on our shoulders. We'd seen the departure of a whole bunch of seniors but had some quality juniors stepping up, and we wanted to see how they'd perform. We were determined to win it all in 2016.

As our scrimmage against New Prague progressed, I kept seeing cheap shots and late hits after the whistle—blatant penalties that went uncalled. My players told me about the fucked-up things New Prague players were saying to them on the field. The N-word was flying, and so were the monkey sounds for which the school had become famous. I instructed my guys to keep their heads down and just play football. I had three kids on probation at the time, two of them wearing ankle bracelets, and we couldn't afford to get caught up in too much mess. Meanwhile, complaints from my players kept rolling in.

Things reached a crescendo when our top receiver, Isaac Johnson, caught a long touchdown pass. Their guys had been riding him all game long—not necessarily racist stuff, but relentless smack talk about how he wouldn't have a good game against

them. Well, after that TD, Isaac looked toward their sideline
with an I-guess-y'all-were-wrong expression.

That's when a New Prague coach strode to the middle of the
field, stuck out his hand toward Isaac, and said, "You're a hell of
a player." Based on everything that had gone down to that point,
I couldn't tell whether the coach was mocking him. It didn't
much matter to me. That's not the kind of thing a coach should
do on the field in the middle of a game.

Isaac ignored the guy entirely and just kept walking. Good.
At that point, the coach turned toward his sideline and said,
loud enough for everybody to hear, "See guys? I told you he was
a jerk." His players started laughing. That was all I needed to
hear. I stormed up to that coach and got into his face. "Don't you
ever speak to one of my kids like that," I said. "How dare you try
to humiliate a young man in front of other people for the sake of
a cheap laugh? You should be ashamed of yourself." My tone was
the same as if I'd been reprimanding one of my own children.
He didn't have much of a response.

The game continued, and so did the late hits. By that point
I was all over the refs. Somebody was going to get hurt. On one
play the ref blew a quick whistle when our running back—Jamin,
the kid who's now in prison—got wrapped up by a defender.
Jamin stopped dead in his tracks, but their guys continued to
play, three of them combining to drive him backward and then
slam him to the ground. Holy shit. I turned toward my dad,
who gave me a nod. My boys were ready to explode, and I wasn't
willing to see what might happen if they stayed on that field for

even one more play. I blew my whistle and shouted to my play-ers, "Get to the bus! *Now!*"

The scrimmage organizer raced over and asked what I was doing. "It's getting too chippy out there, and I don't want any-thing bad to happen this far from home," I told him. "I'm remov-ing my team from this situation." It was the last scrimmage of our day, so I wasn't leaving anybody hanging.

Me and the players talked about it on the drive back to North. We kept talking about it once we arrived. I told my boys to take the energy from whatever feelings had arisen and put it into accomplishing what we'd fallen short of a season ear-lier. "This is how you're going to be treated," I said. "Instead of stooping to the level of teams trying to antagonize us, we have to focus on getting better." I'm not much for kumbaya sessions about why New Prague had treated us like shit—I just wanted to use that anger for fuel moving forward.

About a week later, the head coach at Glencoe emailed me. He'd received a bunch of unsubstantiated complaints from the New Prague coach, he said, and the guy was refusing to partic-ipate in any future scrimmages if North was involved. Without investigating a thing, the coach wrote, "I know you guys have been coming here for years, but I'm sorry, we can't have you back. We received too many complaints from New Prague."

It didn't bother me a bit. "We weren't planning on coming back anyway," I replied. "New Prague talked racist shit to our boys and tried like hell to instigate incidents on the field. I don't want anything to do with that."

Well, things actually worked out for us in the end . . . sort
of. A group of Glencoe parents who'd watched the scrimmage
sent me their own email, saying they heard about their coach's
decision to not invite us back. They wanted to let me know that
from their point of view, the Polars had handled our business
perfectly, not only in that game but across each of the three
years we'd been attending scrimmages there. Everything with
the Polars is yes sir, yes ma'am, thank you sir, thank you ma'am,
they wrote. They said they were appreciative of that. They also
wrote how they watched New Prague try to stir up trouble. If
we're going to ban a team, they said, it should be New Prague.
They wanted North to return. Mind you, this message was from
a group representing a high school that is less than 1 percent
Black.

It was nice to hear, and sure enough, the organizer tried to
get us back the next year. Oh, hell no. You're going to tell me to
my face that the Black team was the problem when every bit of
evidence in front of you says we were actually the victims, and
then try to make nice later? Thanks, but I'm good.

Remember when I said we had three players on probation, two
of them with ankle bracelets? That's not the norm for our football program, but it's also not unusual. I've had a few kids get
into serious trouble over the years (yeah, we've learned how to
thoroughly tape those ankle bracelets), but if I'm being honest,
I can barely tell the difference between the kids in the justice

system and everybody else. I hold my players equally accountable. To me, football is a way to a respectable life. I do all I can to make sure players understand their responsibilities to team and community, and that the way they conduct themselves outside of school can have a dramatic effect on what they do on the field.

In 2016, we turned the idea of responsibility more inward than it had ever been. Tyler Johnson and the players who had come to North with him were graduated and gone, but we had a lot of holdover talent from the 2015 team.

I'd learned some lessons from our loss to Minneota. I'd been too stubborn with our scheme, figuring that it was up to *them* to stop *us*. We've got to be physical, I told my players then, and somehow thought that would be enough. Well, in the playoffs, every team is physical. To put your kids in the best position to succeed you have to coach to the player, not to the scheme. You adapt to them, not the other way around.

After 2015, my focus was on being unified, dividing attention to a host of really good players up and down the roster. I spread the wealth with my play calls, with the goal of making our opponents feel like the only way to beat North was by stopping every single one of us. For me, the shift was as simple as asking who would be our player of the game, every game, and never knowing the answer until it was over.

The Polars' 2016 season started off with a bang, and not in a good way. Our second possession of our first game, against Washburn, ended in a massive brawl. Our punter, Ahzerik "Zeke" Rodgers—who I was about to insert as quarterback— was leveled after his punt had already bounced out of bounds, by a player who wasn't even in the game. It was a truly violent hit that caught Zeke completely unaware. One of our linemen, Jamire Jackson, came in throwing punches, and soon a scrum of players was brawling. Parents jumped out of the stands, though they were prevented from joining in the fight.

It took nearly a half hour to break that thing up and get my team back to our side of the field. Before we ran another play, I huddled with the opposing coach, various assistant coaches, and our respective athletic directors. For me, the path forward was clear. "Nobody's scored yet, so fuck it, let's end this game right now," I said. "If we're going to start our season like this, we may as well just call it a day."

Thankfully, Reggie Perkins, the athletic director at Washburn, was there. I'd first heard of Reggie during his time playing for St. Cloud State and then the Harlem Globetrotters. I got to know him personally when he became a JV basketball coach at North. Now, at midfield, Reggie didn't mince words. "Charles, I understand how you feel, but ending this game because of fighting will look bad for our district and our city," he said. "It'll send the message that we can't even get our shit together to finish a football game." The man had a point.

Reggie suggested the teams split the blame equally, and that we continue the game. Each roster ended up with two players ejected, though it could have been many more on each side. For us it was Zeke and Jamire, and that was a pretty steep price to pay: ejection meant suspension from the following game as well, so those guys ended up missing nearly two full games.

It didn't make much difference on the scoreboard. We beat Washburn by seven, then won our next game 38–0, thanks to three punt-return touchdowns. The following game I installed Zeke as QB, and he threw three TD passes. Jamire came back and led the team with twelve tackles. We needed them because starting that game we were without another of our best players, thanks to some drama that would take the rest of the season to fully play out.

It started with a report I received about how our best pass rusher and lead receiver, Isaac Johnson, had already racked up thirteen class tardies less than a month into the school year. I request those kinds of updates from teachers because I have methods for keeping kids in line. If I hear about behavioral issues, your ass is on the bench—for a series, for multiple series, for a quarter, or for a game. For small-time infractions like tardies, my long-standing policy involves a one-hundred-yard pre-practice sprint for every time you've been late to class. That's if you're lucky. If you're unlucky, you get a nom. (Should you ever encounter a North High Polar who played under me, mention the word "nom" and see what kind of reaction you get.) A nom involves a one-hundred-yard sprint to the far end of the field, a bear crawl back to the beginning, a duck-walk to the opposite end, and then the true killer: kids have to roll the remaining hundred yards to the finish line. Noms are strictly an end-of-practice punishment because it's impossible for players to be productive afterward. I've never seen anyone do more than one.

I didn't make Isaac give me any noms, but I did tell him he couldn't touch the practice field until I received one length of sprints for each tardy—1,300 yards in all. If I'm being honest, one reason my teams are so effective in the fourth quarter of games is that we're in shape, and we're in shape partly because we do so much punitive running. Well, Isaac started off on his laps. He did one. I watched him. Then he went straight to the receivers line to get his reps.

"What are you doing?" I said. "You gotta finish your run."

"I did," he insisted. "I ran thirteen hundred yards."

No way. "You don't touch the ball until you finish running," I said. Before I knew what was happening I was in the middle of an argument I shouldn't have been in at all.

"Fuck it," he yelled to me and the heavens both. "I quit!"

Now I was pissed. "Go ahead," I said. "It's up to you."

Isaac grabbed his stuff and stormed off the field. His biggest mistake came as he passed by the golf cart where I was sitting, when he threw his dirty, sweaty jersey at me. Then he did the unthinkable.

"You fucking pig," he spat.

That is one thing you do not say to a cop. Isaac had never been in trouble with the law and didn't hold any grudges against the police as far as I knew. He was just trying to get under my skin. It worked. I'd never been so angry at a player in my life. Isaac was only a teenager, but he was a *big* teenager—six-foot-three and two hundred pounds. I grabbed him by his collar, held him up, and got nose to nose with him. Before anything else could happen, my dad raced over and yelled at both of us to knock it the hell off. That stopped me in my tracks. I pushed Isaac away.

"Get off my field!" I shouted. Thankfully, he did.

Not ten minutes later, Isaac's father, Ken Johnson, showed up. He was an assistant coach on the basketball team and had been in the gym. Isaac told him about what happened, and his dad wanted to hear it from me. As I thought about it, I had plenty of reasons to be angry, but I'd also taken things too far. I explained the entire incident and added regret for putting my hands on his son. "That part was uncalled for," I said.

Ken was understanding. "You're like another father to him," he said. "I'm sure he pushed you to this."

That respect, one coach to another, made me feel good. Here was somebody with reason to be angry who gave me the benefit of the doubt. It pushed me no closer to reconciling with Isaac, though. He'd lied, quit, said hurtful things, and stormed away. Allowing him back onto the roster would require a conversation. I needed to hear him express some accountability. Trouble was, Isaac didn't want to talk, and if Isaac didn't own his actions, he wasn't about to play. This was not something I would bend on. If one kid got away with that behavior, it would set a terrible example for the rest of the team. If we couldn't win without Isaac, it was a price I was willing to pay.

To Isaac's credit, he showed up at games and supported the team from just off the sidelines. He'd been part of a group of players who regularly ate lunch in my office, and for a few weeks he was a no-show there, laying low in a clear effort to avoid me. One day, though, he shuffled in with the usual gang, unpacked his food, and carried on like nothing had happened. That was okay by me. I wasn't about to kick him out.

After three or four games, various groups of players came to discuss the possibility of allowing Isaac to return. I'm pretty sure Isaac put them up to it, but that didn't invalidate their feelings— he was their guy, and they wanted him on the field. It was a collaborative effort, and it didn't work. That was the wrong formula to change my mind.

Eventually Isaac went to my sister Brittney, who was a dean at North High at the time, and asked her to intercede on his behalf. Her advice was for him to bring lunch into my office, apologize, and agree to talk things through. She knew that was the only possible path. Isaac did exactly that.

In my office, he told me that he was sorry for his behavior. I listened and nodded. We hugged it out. I was ready to accept Isaac's words on a personal level but not from a football standpoint. I still had a team to coach, and Isaac, an unquestioned team leader, had set a horrible example. In my mind, letting him return would be an endorsement of bad behavior. It also went against my theme for the season, which was to focus on the collective, not on individual players. "I forgive you Isaac," I told him, "but I can't let you come back. Not yet." I wasn't sure what it would take for me to relent. I just knew I wasn't feeling it at that moment.

"I respect that, Coach," he said. "I get it."

Even without Isaac, we continued to win. Victories on the road at Ashland and Spectrum. A divisional blowout over Roosevelt. A shutout against Edison. We ran off seven straight wins to head into our season finale undefeated. That game, against St. Agnes, marked an important progression for us thanks to my granddaddy's brother—my great-uncle, Jimmy Adams. Jimmy was a legendary high school football coach in East St. Louis, a literal hall of famer. When I was a kid, whenever my dad went to visit him, he'd return with a duffel bag full of equipment: helmets, shoulder pads, knee braces. I used that stuff for years.

The weekend before the season ended, Jimmy came to Minneapolis to attend my dad's wedding to his second wife, Carol. We all gathered at Dad's condo for dinner that Saturday night, at which point Jimmy asked what kind of defense North was running. I called up some film on my phone, and we gathered around the dining room table to watch it. Jimmy was a downright guru with that kind of stuff, and I was eager to hear his opinion. It took him only moments to speak up.

"Y'all fucked up." That was the first thing out of his mouth. If nothing else, the man was candid.

We'd been running a 5–3 formation—five linemen to rush the passer, with three linebackers in the space behind them to react to whatever might happen. It had served us well—the Polars had given up only three scores across our last three games—but it really was the most basic rec league defense out there, and it limited our ability to blitz. Still, it was what my defensive coordinator wanted, and I hadn't messed with it too much.

Jimmy had me pause the film. "The problem is, you fuckers are predictable, which is why you're getting your asses kicked," he said. Jimmy really liked to curse. Also, he was right. We hadn't lost a game, but truth was, teams *were* scoring on us. Two of our wins were by only a touchdown, and four opponents had scored in double figures. A year earlier we'd given up twenty points *all season.*

Jimmy reached across the table for a napkin and drew up a defensive scheme. As he explained his diagram, I understood the truth behind every word he said. Going back to our loss to Minneota in the previous season's title game, we'd noticed that pressing with a linebacker meant that we had nobody at the second level if the ball carrier broke through. As my uncle, my dad, and I talked it over, it became clear that our current defense was good enough against pedestrian opponents, but we'd lost the championship game because it couldn't hold up against an elite offense. Minneota's 2015 title was their second in a row, and they were undefeated in their 2016 follow-up campaign, as good as ever. Jimmy was right. We needed a change. Thankfully, Jimmy himself was there to lend insight.

"You need to put your kids in better positions," he said. That's exactly what I'd been doing for the offense. Why not the defense, too? The scheme he suggested, a 4-2-5, allowed us to drop linemen into coverage and occasionally task cornerbacks—the guys ordinarily responsible for covering wide receivers—with rushing the passer. This offered a diversity of looks that confused the hell out of quarterbacks. We could run man-to-man or Cover 3 out of the same look. I took over the defensive play-calling myself and installed a ton of crazy blitzes—double A gaps, B gaps, stunts. Our guys were all over the field. The players *loved* that defense. We named it "St. Louis" in honor of Jimmy's roots.

We unveiled it against St. Agnes, and it ate them up. Their first play was a pass directly to our defender, who returned it for a touchdown. Our final score of the day came on another interception return. In between, we picked off two more passes, forced a fumble, and sacked the quarterback six times. The 38–14 score didn't begin to show how dominant we'd been.

I would have been more excited about things had our lead running back, Ty'ree Cox, not torn his ACL. Ty'ree was a senior, and he looked like an NFL star against St. Agnes: twenty-two rushes for 172 yards and two TDs, plus two of our four interceptions as a cornerback. Late in the game, as he fought for an extra yard, he got tackled awkwardly and his knee snapped. As his teammates helped him off the field, I was faced with a startling reality: Ty'ree had been our best player since Isaac left the team, and losing him at the start of our playoff run was devastating. There was lots of talent on the depth chart behind him, but for a team with championship aspirations, his absence was meaningful. Could we hang with Minneota minus Isaac *and* Ty'ree? I was far from certain.

As it turned out, much of my roster shared that mindset. Prior to our first game of the section tournament, against Kerkhoven, two players, Nas El-Amin and Tayler Johnson (Tyler's younger brother), came to see me, urging me to reinstate Isaac for the playoffs. "We need him," Nas said. He wasn't wrong. As a defensive end, Isaac was unblockable, and as a receiver he could both stretch the field and catch balls across the middle.

It didn't matter. I wasn't budging. "Isaac was disrespectful," I told them. "If we're going to win this thing, we'll win it the right way."

Then Tayler piped up. "Stop making this about you, Coach," he said. That was a bold statement. It took a while for the message to sink in, but I eventually understood his point. Suspending Isaac had been entirely about his behavior, but keeping him out so long might be a different matter. I held firm, though. Even players as good as Isaac could not be so disrespectful and then just return to the team as if everything was okay. The lesson might be learned at some point, but we weren't there yet.

As it happened, we didn't need Isaac in the section tournament. Kehyan Porter, who'd barely played all season, started his first game at the varsity level against Kerkhoven in place of Ty'ree. He ran for 265 yards and three touchdowns, averaging nearly 10 yards per clip. My new focus on the entire roster instead of just a few star players was paying off. After we closed out a 40–14 victory, I turned to my dad on the sideline. "Well," I said, "I think that solves our running back issue."

As I walked off the field amid our celebrating players, out of the corner of my eye I spotted Isaac, just off the sideline as usual. He shook his head and smiled. I could *feel* him wishing he had been on that field. I made a mental note. Maybe he really had learned his lesson.

That night I went to my dad's house. My mom was in town from St. Augustine, Florida, where she'd moved a couple of years earlier. For the first time since we were kids, she and Dad were hanging out together. My brother and sister were also there. Mom cooked dinner. We were all sitting around the living room, just like old times, when I got an alert on my phone: Minneota had lost to Wabasso. I'd been gearing up to beat those guys all season long, and now they were out of the tournament. I could hardly believe it.

"Dad! Dad! Minneota lost!" I shouted. He read the game details over my shoulder, and we both sat quietly with our new reality for a moment. Dad broke the silence with an order.

"Call Isaac right now," he said. "We're gonna win the whole damn thing."

My first instinct was to reject the suggestion outright. To call Isaac because an opportunity had opened up was to concede whatever moral high ground I'd been trying to claim. My father, however, knew better. He'd been giving me leeway to handle the situation however I saw fit, and now was the time for him to step in.

"Spanky, I saw him at the game," he told me. "I saw his face. He's clearly sorry for whatever happened. At this point, holding him out is about you, not him. Six games is penalty enough. We need him." Wow. That was the second time in a couple weeks that somebody told me to not make this about me. I'd also seen Isaac, and I agreed with my dad: he did look sorry.

"Call Isaac," Dad said again. "Call him now."

I was the head coach, but he was my father. My first step was to check in with my other assistants, to see if any of them had concerns. They did not. So I did as Dad instructed. I picked up the phone.

"Hey Coach, what's up?" Isaac said when he got on the line.

The first thing out of my mouth was, "Man, if I let you come back . . ."

I didn't even get to finish the sentence. "Coach, I'll do whatever you ask me to," he yelped.

I gave Isaac my ground rules. He had to apologize to the coaches and his teammates, and he would be on a tight leash when it came to his behavior. He agreed. The next day at practice, Isaac stood in front of the team and told them he was sorry both for quitting and putting them in the position he did. We hadn't lost a game without him, but he said he still felt like he let the team down and that it wouldn't happen again.

Then he ran the 1,200 yards of sprints he still owed me.

Was I too tough on Isaac? Probably. I think my dad and Tayler were right—I made the situation unnecessarily personal. Still, I am adamant about modeling good behavior, and one of the best ways to do that is by holding players accountable. Maybe I should have let Isaac return a couple of games earlier, but I'll say this much for my tactics: the lesson stuck. After high school, Isaac played Division I basketball at Western Illinois. "OA, you put the team before me," he told me a couple of years after he graduated. "Nobody had ever stood up to me like that before. That was the best thing I could have gone through."

From the moment I reinstated Isaac, he was a terror on the field. He'd used his time off constructively, staying focused and in shape, and he came back more mature. A victory in our next game, against Mayer Lutheran, would qualify us for the state tournament, and Isaac was a beast, all but unblockable at defensive end, getting into the quarterback's face almost as soon as the ball was snapped. In fact, the guy was so quick to the line that he kept jumping offside. My dad, coordinating the defense from the press box, didn't mind. He noticed that the quarterback spent most of his pre-snap reads nervously eyeing Isaac, literally shaking so much that Dad could see it in the booth. He radioed down to the sideline. "Their quarterback is scared to death," he said. "Give Isaac a green light to jump offside if it helps him time the snap. I want to scare this dude. Tell him to *go!*"

We demolished that team, 46–12, Isaac marking his return not only with defensive disruption but catching six balls for ninety-seven yards and two touchdowns. For the third season in a row we were headed to the state tournament.

This seems like a good spot to talk about my assistant coaches. The obvious place to start is with my father. Dad was smart enough to tell me when to reinstate Isaac, and I was smart enough to listen. I can't say for sure that I would have taken his advice had it come from anybody else.

When I took over at North for the second time, the team's coordinators were already in place, so Dad just started showing up to help out however he could. He eventually took over the defensive secondary, coaching cornerbacks and safeties. Dad had no high school coaching experience, but he knew football and how to reach young men. The fact that he was my father didn't hurt when it came to earning players' respect.

Whenever we talk to people about our on-field relationship, Dad makes sure to note that I'm the boss . . . yet he'll occasionally lay into me in front of the players with jokes like, "If you cross me, you'll get a whooping." The kids love hearing that, but the truth is that while Dad suggests all sorts of things, he never tries to overrule me. Coordinators and position coaches are not always on board with the head coach's plan. That's just football. Some even undermine directives they don't like. That's never been the case with Dad.

My father and I occasionally get into it, of course. Waylaid by police duties, he once arrived shortly before halftime to a game in which I had just backed the safeties up to prevent a long pass. When the whistle sounded, the coaches huddled together before heading into the locker room for the break. He lit into me, pissed off. "You shouldn't have done that with the safeties," he said. "*I* wouldn't have done that."

"Then you should have been here on time," I shot back.

We went at it like that for a few moments, until I decided I'd had enough. "You know what?" I said to the rest of the coaches. "This motherfucker is fired. I need a new DB coach."

"You're firing me?" Dad said, incredulous. "Okay, then." With that, he took off his belt.

The other coaches, enjoying this interplay tremendously, play-held him back, but Dad broke free and began whacking me while our players waited patiently in the end zone with little idea what was going on. My staff was in tears from laughing so hard.

That my dad is also police adds another layer of authority to the coaching staff. He's not the only one. I seem to attract cops to my ranks, especially recently. My dad was first, of course. Next came Tim Lawrence, our offensive line coach, who I hired less because he wears blue—he's a lieutenant with the Metro Transit Police Department—and more because he'd played college ball at Bethel University and really knew his stuff.

The most recent cop is also my longest-tenured assistant, Rick Plunkett, who was the offensive coordinator when I first came on board and is still around, having filled several positions over the years. Rick is a North Minneapolis guy, a Park Center Senior High School alum, and a neighborhood barber. Rick has been cutting my hair since before we started coaching together. In 2019, he became a patrolman in the First Precinct. He'd been considering that career change for a long while; proximity to the rest of us cops on the coaching staff helped move the decision along. Our assistant receivers coach, Cordarelle Scales, is in the process of applying to become an officer, and our defensive line coach, Lance Horton, used to work in the jail system and is now in corporate security. Defensive coordinator Claude Labossiere has worked in a number of correctional facilities across Minnesota and now provides security at Children's Hospital in Minneapolis.

Fielding a staff filled with law-enforcement officers doesn't necessarily make for a better football program, but it certainly doesn't hurt. There is a lot of overlap between what we do professionally and what we bring to the field. Discipline is common to both areas, and working with people who understand the concept helps maintain order during practices and games. Far more important than the football piece is the community piece. All of us officer/coaches provide players the kind of positive interaction with law enforcement that they might not otherwise get, which allows us a profound degree of communication that would otherwise be inaccessible. Benefits flow in both directions. My single greatest strength as SRO at North was that because students trusted me as a person, they trusted me as a policeman, which in turn helped me do my job more efficiently and effectively. The same dynamic plays out to varying degrees across members of my staff, each of whom is able to deeply connect to the community through high school football. It's a good template.

Of course, not everyone on my staff wears blue (apart from our Polars gear). My longtime assistant head coach, Tom Lachermeier, heads the history department at North High and has been divvying up the offensive coordinator duties with Rick for years. Craig Merritt has been North's JV coach since a year or two after I came on board. He not only played down the line from me as a wide receiver on my own Polars team back in the day, but also in the Park Board league when we were kids. We've been friends for more than thirty years. Other key coaches over the years include Kyle Fox, an assistant DB coach who I met through the Fellowship of Christian Athletes; special teams coach Beulah Lee Verdell, a professional nurse who keeps stats for us and does our game write-ups; and Kriss Burrell (our get-back coach, in charge of making sure our sideline group stays the requisite distance from the field of play), who is a dean at North High.

I've said it many times, including within these pages: without coaches like these to handle the day-to-day, I would be less able to spend as much time as I do looking after the overall health of the program and players alike, which to me is the most essential aspect of my job.

Chapter 7

Polar Pride

When it comes to high school football in Minnesota, the state tournament is everything, the big stage, where you get to play in top facilities and on television. College coaches use these games to identify recruitment targets. Every year my players put up scholarship-worthy numbers, but the only time college reps seem to pay attention to us is when we play under that spotlight. I cannot overstate how vital the state tournament is to a program like North's.

The Polars appeared there three times before I became head coach and each time were quickly eliminated. We made it again in 2014, Tyler Johnson's junior year, and won our first-round game. In 2015, we advanced to the championship, losing to Minneota.

It took only one game in 2016, our state tournament opener, for me to know we were going to win it all.

It was against Janesville-Waldorf-Pemberton, at night, in 30-degree weather. Yeah, we're from Minnesota and are used to playing in inclement conditions, but it doesn't feel good to get beaten when it's freezing outside. Which is exactly what was happening. We had the ball for all of five plays in the first quarter, and at halftime we trailed 13–0. Officials gave us the option to head indoors to the locker room for the break. Janesville elected to remain outside, which made some sense—their players kept moving to stay warm, and they wouldn't have to reacclimatize when play resumed. Me? I went inside with my team. I'd like to say it was a master stroke of preparatory genius, but really I just had to pee.

When I emerged from the bathroom, I found the team sitting quietly, waiting to hear whatever words of wisdom I might have put together for them. I stared at them. They stared back.

Finally somebody piped up: "Don't you have something to say?"

Nah. Not now.

"Shit man, I don't have any big thoughts for you," I told the players. "I brought y'all in here because I had to take a piss. If you want inspiration or some new strategy, you'll be waiting a while because you don't need it. If you think thirteen points is going to beat you, then you're already beaten. Do I seem worried? Shit, let's just go out there and score some points."

Then I walked back outside, into the cold.

This was no kick-the-water-bottles moment. They couldn't believe I wasn't angry. The reason I wasn't angry was because I believed everything I'd said. No way was a thirteen-point deficit going to hold this team back. If we stuck to our game plan, I was confident that everything would turn out just fine.

Which is exactly what happened. The third quarter started in earnest when Odell Wilson, a junior defensive lineman, sacked their quarterback for a twenty-yard loss to force a punt, which Jamin then returned thirty-four yards for a touchdown. A two-point conversion made it 13–8. On Janesville's very next play, Isaac forced a fumble that we recovered. Zeke followed by zipping a ten-yard touchdown pass to Corleone Powell. Only six minutes had elapsed, and North led 16–13. We were just getting started.

Kehyan Porter punched one in from the two-yard line. Isaac ran another one in from fourteen yards out. We intercepted two more passes and sacked the quarterback five times. In all we put up four unanswered touchdowns to win the game, 32–13. Afterward, reporters asked what I'd said to my kids at halftime. I sure didn't cop to the shortest pep talk in history: "I had to take a piss."

Starting with that comeback, those North kids truly believed they could become champions. Soon enough, they would be.

After our victory against Janesville-Waldorf-Pemberton, the only thing standing between us and the championship game was the semifinal against Wabasso, the team that had beaten

Minneota. This was big for us because it was at U.S. Bank Stadium in downtown Minneapolis, the brand-new home of the Vikings that's only a ten-minute drive from North High.

Wabasso fielded a Minnesota Mr. Football Award candidate, a do-everything running back who people said we wouldn't be able to stop. I wasn't so sure they were wrong. We'd seen this formula before, though, with our own roster a year earlier. Minneota had stopped Tyler Johnson, or at least slowed him down enough to win, and we'd had no response. Now, though, I was able to tell my team, "They have one guy but we have fifty, and they'll have to stop all fifty of us to win."

That's pretty much how it worked out.

Their running back racked up 105 yards on the day, but it took him twenty-five rushes to get there. Apart from a 41-yard touchdown run, we held him to 2.7 yards per carry, and he was more or less all they had. The Polars sacked Wabasso's quarterback four times and held their offense to seven total yards in the third quarter. On our side of the ball, Kehyan Porter gave us 118 rushing yards on only sixteen carries—a number that would have been much higher had he not gotten tripped up on an 80-yard run just before halftime and hit his head on the turf. He couldn't finish, so I put in Jamin, who collected 79 rushing yards of his own, including a 12-yard touchdown run in the third quarter.

There's a reason Wabasso had beaten Minneota. They were good. The Wabasso defense clamped down, and after Jamin's TD, neither team scored through the rest of the third quarter and into the fourth. We led only 16–8, and while we weren't giving anything to Wabasso, they weren't giving anything to us, either. I was anxious, and with Kehyan concussed and Ty'ree out with an ACL injury, I began to panic. I started nagging my coaches on the sideline. "We gotta figure something out," I kept saying. "This shit ain't working." That led to one of the best moments of the season for me. My offensive coordinator, Tom Lachermeier, who was calling plays from the press box, set me straight. "Don't start that shit now," he barked into my headset. "You've trusted us all year. Be patient. We *have* this."

Tom was effectively saying, "Unless you want to call the plays yourself, shut up and let us do our job." It's funny because just a week earlier my whole halftime talk had been, "If y'all think thirteen points is gonna beat you . . ." As is frequently the case, Tom was right. I did as he said and trusted our system. Sure enough, our lead held up. Wabasso had a chance to tie it with a Hail Mary pass on their final play, but Tayler intercepted it and the celebration began. We were one win from North's first-ever state football championship.

Rushford-Peterson was a good team with a great player, Noah Carlson, who was widely considered to be the best prep athlete in Minnesota. That spring he won state track championships in the 200, the long jump, and the triple jump, and went on to join the University of Michigan track team. As a running back he was our division's Associated Press football player of the year, based in part because he averaged 190 rushing yards per game with nearly three touchdowns per. During the state tournament he'd upped that number to more than 230 yards per game. If the Wabasso kid we'd faced a week earlier was good, Noah was jaw-dropping. In the week leading up to the championship, all the talk seemed to center on how North wouldn't be able to contain him. Rushford was a nearly unanimous favorite among the local media.

The Polars took that as motivation.

We started on defense, and on the second play of the game, I called for a double A gap blitz in which both linebackers were supposed to crash on either side of the center. For it to work, our defensive end had to cover the B gap between the guard and the tackle. That's not how it worked out. Our end got caught inside, and our linebackers ran into each other. Carlson was savvy enough to burst through the opening that was created, running past our entire defense and breaking multiple tackles en route to a seventy-four-yard touchdown. The stadium went crazy. It was not the start we were hoping for.

When I watched the replay on the big screen, though, I saw that even with our mistakes we'd still nearly stopped him cold. My dad, running the defense from the press box, saw the same thing. "I'm not worried," he said to me over the radio. It wasn't much, but reassuring words from your father can go a long way.

They intercepted Zeke in their own end zone on our first real drive, and we didn't make it back there until the second quarter. At that point, with the ball at Rushford's thirteen-yard line, we sent Nas El-Amin underneath and Isaac in motion in the same direction. Their defense flocked, leaving Tayler

Johnson wide open behind them in the end zone. Zeke's pass was on the money. Touchdown. A two-point conversion gave us an 8–7 lead.

Rushford's next possession was vital for us in multiple ways. They'd done little more than feed it to Carlson all game long, and apart from his long run we'd done a good job bottling him up. On his sixth run of the drive, he was hit hard at the line by our defensive end, Phillip Scott, who at six-foot-three and 230 pounds was the strongest guy on our team. Phillip dislodged the ball, and Tayler scooped it up, returning it sixty yards for his second touchdown in just over three minutes, extending our lead to 14–7. Of more lasting importance, during our ensuing, successful two-point conversion, Isaac, defended by Carlson, leaped for a pass and inadvertently landed on Noah's leg. Carlson stayed in the game (he caught a short touchdown just before halftime to close the score to 16–14), but he was clearly injured.

With under a minute left in the half, Zeke fumbled inside our twenty, and Rushford recovered. Two Carlson rushes brought them to our one-yard line with time for one more play. As their quarterback took the snap, he fell backward and lost control of the ball. Isaac was right there to pick it up. No Rushford player was near him as he started down the field toward what looked like a certain score . . . until the play was whistled dead. The ref ruled that Rushford's QB was down before he fumbled, but we were playing in an NFL stadium with an NFL scoreboard and saw the replay immediately. The QB was *not* down, and I wasn't the only one who knew it. As we departed the field for halftime, an official approached me apologetically. "Sorry, Coach, we fucked that one up," he said. That should have been a touchdown for us. Because the guy admitted they had blown it, I couldn't even argue with him, which made me even angrier.

As we walked toward the locker room, a sideline reporter for the TV broadcast was waiting for me. "Coach Adams, how do you think you did?" she said. I was in a state over the call, and ended up taking out my frustration on her. I barked at that poor lady for the duration of our interview, which I didn't even realize until I saw the clip later on. She handled it perfectly. "Love the passion from Coach Adams—you wouldn't think his team is winning right now," she said as she tossed it upstairs.

(That wouldn't be the game's only blown call to take points off the board for us. In the second half, Kehyan hit the pylon on a two-point conversion, but even though the big-screen replay kept showing otherwise, the ref said he was out of bounds. As if that wasn't enough, the next day's sports page had a photo of Kehyan, in bounds, scoring. Take that, ref.)

In case I wasn't irritated enough about the way the first half ended, as the Polars entered the tunnel I saw the champion and runner-up trophies on display. Somehow the first-place trophy already had Rushford-Peterson's picture in it. Can you believe that? It was all the inspiration I needed for my halftime speech. I burst into the locker room and began yelling.

"Them motherfuckers don't want us to win!" I shouted, pointing toward the door. "Rushford's picture is already in the trophy case!" I went nuts with that speech, which, unlike my kicking of the water bottle carrier, featured genuine rage.

"They say y'all can't stop Noah, but I'll tell you this: if Noah gets another motherfucking yard, all y'all motherfuckers will be walking home. He better not get *another fucking yard*." Sometimes a well-placed curse word or six can really hit home.

"Yeah, Coach! Yeah!" the kids cheered.

"Y'all heard me?" I said. "Now let's go kick their asses!"

I've never seen a more hyped group of players in my life. They raced out of that locker room like their jocks were on fire, ready to grind whatever came between them and that championship into dust.

As my dad and I followed them out, we passed Rushford-Peterson's locker room. The door was open, and we saw Noah Carlson on the training table. He looked up, our eyes met, and his expression gave away everything. He couldn't take much more. Our defenders had swarmed him relentlessly and hit him hard, and he'd clearly injured something during that play with Isaac. He was breaking down. Rushford had run twenty-nine plays in the first half, including twenty Carlson rushes, three passes to Carlson, and one pass *by* Carlson. Apart from his huge first run, the guy had totaled forty-four yards on the ground and fumbled the ball away. Me and my dad both saw it in his face. "His ass is done," Dad said as we walked onto the field.

Rushford-Peterson's first possession of the second half began with two handoffs to Carlson, who gained a combined twenty-two yards. They would be his last significant gains of the day, the remainder of which consisted of five more rushes for negative-one yard. Whatever success Noah had had in the first half was simply nonexistent in the second half. Rushford didn't even run the ball on their last possession.

Well, we came to find out that Noah's injury was more severe than anybody realized. He hadn't just tweaked something—he'd broken his damn leg. We learned the details during basketball season, when North played Rushford and Noah showed up in a cast. It turns out I'd read his expression perfectly, but the kid had more reason for his defeated look than I understood. He ended up rushing twenty-seven times for 161 yards in that championship game while playing half of it on a broken leg. He never came out. It was freaking heroic.

Meanwhile, our defense shut Rushford down entirely in the second half, holding them to sixteen plays across four possessions, including three punts. On offense, Kehyan ran one in from eight yards out, and Zeke tossed a thirteen-yard touchdown to Jamin in the fourth quarter, making it 30–14. When Jamire Jackson intercepted a pass with just under two minutes to go, we were ready to celebrate.

As the clock ran down, I noticed just how anxious I was. That's when I truly realized we were about to become state champions. My dad, who'd spent the game up in the booth, came down with a couple of minutes remaining to be with me on the sidelines. So did my son, Adrian, who was in tenth grade and not yet on the varsity team; he served as the ball boy that day. We weren't allowed Gatorade jugs on the sideline, so players dumped cups of water on me. I hugged Adrian and cried. My dad was emotional, too. When I looked into the stands, I saw it wasn't just him—so were my wife, daughters, uncles, and aunts. Out of nowhere, my phone rang. It was Tyler Johnson, by then a freshman at the University of Minnesota, calling with congratulations. Given that my whole family was there in the building with me, Tyler might have been the only person on the planet for whom I'd actually pick up. He was as giddy as if he'd been on that field himself. Everybody understood the gravity of the moment. A reporter from 45TV raced over. "You're the first African American coach ever to win a state football title," she said. "What does that mean to you?"

"That means there've got to be more Black coaches who win, because I'm trying to go every year," I said, referring to the championship game. "Feel me?"

More than any of that, I was happy for my players and for the Northside. Of the eight teams in the state tournament, we were the only one from Minneapolis proper. Everyone in the city was looking toward us.

Now I'm seeing alumni in the crowd. I'm seeing former teammates, people I went to school with. I realize that the whole city is there to support me and these boys, and we've accomplished something to make everybody proud. Nobody in those stands had ever seen a championship from this school or this community. We gave that to them.

That victory was one of my greatest moments. Like my dad once told me, winning isn't everything, but losing ain't shit. I was presented a gold helmet as a trophy, and I gave it to Dad, who keeps it in his office at the Fourth Precinct.

*   *   *

If you look at historical pictures of Minnesota state championship football teams, you'll see an awful lot of pale faces. Team
after team after team is entirely white. Only two state champions in Minnesota history have been majority Black, and North
was one of them. That might be because football is on a steady
decline in the city among schools that look like ours. Even Minnesota's rec league system has suffered.

Realistically, our state high school league is not set up for
Black kids from the inner city to succeed. North High currently
plays in Class AA (they bumped us up a division after our championship, even though our enrollment never increased), and to
face a team of any quality we have to do some serious traveling.
In 2021, we drove ninety miles to Rochester for the state tournament quarterfinal. Until the state semifinals, which are held
at the big stadiums in Minneapolis, suburban and rural teams
never come close to our city limits. If we want to play the state's
best competition, we must go to them . . . and it's there that we
encounter the racist epithets and monkey noises that paint our
league in such a poor light. Stop turning the Black kids into sac-
rificial lambs. Stop making them go through that shit every year.

I've recommended that the best way to spotlight inner-city
schools is by giving them their own class within Minneapolis
and St. Paul, combining city teams for our own state tournament. On one hand, it would guarantee that a city team would
be crowned champion every year. Think that's crazy? In 2016,
the Polars were the first Minneapolis City Conference team to
win a state title since 1977, and only the third ever. What better

way to highlight the conference with the largest minority representation in the state than by giving it its own championship? Even more than that, a Twin Cities Conference would eliminate most of our travel, and our teams would get to play in front of people who care about them instead of traveling alone, hours outside town, while family members stay home.

There are plenty of potential host facilities for a Twin Cities league, including an MSL soccer stadium; Concordia University's Division II field in St. Paul; TCF Bank Stadium, home of the Golden Gophers; and the Vikings' field, U.S. Bank Stadium in Minneapolis. There are also fields at Macalester College and Hamline University. Public transportation accesses all of them. Other states have metro leagues—why not Minnesota?

North didn't have to worry about many travel logistics prior to our championship victory. U.S. Bank Stadium is virtually around the corner from our campus, and that short bus ride home was a rolling party. We danced and hugged and took pictures. We pulled into the school parking lot to find an actual party waiting for us in the gym, with catered food and close to a thousand people. We'd had no idea. My guys bounced in with their medals and were treated like the champions they'd become.

I've learned a lot of lessons about how much more difficult it is to remain at those heights than it is to reach them in the first place. North has been back to the championship game once since 2016, which we lost to Caledonia, a longtime Minnesota AA powerhouse.

What's next for our football program? These days, Northside athletic culture is mostly about basketball. Kids feel like failures if they don't succeed on the court, regardless of what happens on the football field. Students transfer out of North because the basketball team is too competitive for them to stand out. They can be all-everything in football, but if they don't cut it as basketball players, they go someplace else. Even after we lost that state football championship in 2015, Tyler told me, "I got you Coach—we're gonna go win it in basketball." Then he and the basketball team did exactly that. The next year, after our football team finally took home a title, the basketball team went out and did it again. Those were some kinds of years for our athletic program.

I remember one practice early in my tenure, when North was struggling with attendance. My father looked around and noted that we probably had more coaches than players . . . and we had only a few coaches. These days we're flush with them. The defensive line has a coach, the linebackers have a coach, and my dad handles the defensive backs. Each of those coaches has assistant coaches. We have a quarterbacks coach, multiple offensive line coaches, a receivers coach, a running backs coach, and a special teams coach. I have a dozen coaches on my varsity staff, and another thirteen between our freshman and JV teams.

"With all these assistants," my dad once observed about my coaching style, "you really don't do shit but stand there and complain."

Just the way I like it.

Chapter 8

Riot

On May 25, 2020, Minneapolis Police officer Derek Chauvin held his knee on the neck of George Floyd, who was lying face down and incapacitated on a sidewalk in South Minneapolis. They were at the corner of Thirty-Eighth Street and Chicago Avenue, a Black and Latino neighborhood lined by minority-owned shops and restaurants. I wouldn't call the place poor, but thanks to gang activity, crime there is abundant. It's like the Northside with different gangs.

I knew Chauvin. We came up as community service officers together in the Third Precinct prior to joining the force. We were in college at the time, working twenty hours per week as glorified gophers so the MPD would pay for our schooling. I did physical training with him as part of a larger group, running three days per week and working out at the athletic club.

I'd volunteered to chaperone a Police Activities League fishing trip to Eddie's Resort that my then-four-year-old son,

Adrian, was signed up for in 2004 or 2005. So did Chauvin. I
didn't know him well, but even through our cursory interactions
I could tell that Derek's personality was . . . different. I heard
he'd been in the military, which made sense; with him, everything was straight and narrow, always at full attention. There
were maybe fifteen CSOs in our group, all of us college students,
and Derek's demeanor always seemed kind of weird to the rest
of us. I think he wanted to fit in, but he was always trying to
portray himself as some sort of authority figure or veteran officer, above everybody else. We ended up at different precincts
so I don't know how he adapted once he officially joined the
force, but in that CSO program he was unmistakably awkward.
Not angry or some of the other traits commentators have since
ascribed to him, just awkward. Different.

Then he choked out George Floyd and everything went
to hell.

I was at home when I heard about it. MPD's public information officer sent a standard notification email about an in-
custody death to everybody in the department. I didn't think
much more about it until later that night, when video surfaced
of George's final moments. I saw it on Facebook, and as I
watched him on the ground under Chauvin's knee, I literally
grew sick to my stomach. You could see the life being sucked
out of him.

Oh shit, I thought, things are going to get bad. People will
be pissed about this. People *should* be pissed about this. At that
moment, I had only a vague sense of where we were headed.

Minneapolis has had our share of police killings over recent years. In 2015, an unarmed twenty-four-year-old named Jamar Clark was shot outside a Northside party only sixty-one seconds after officers arrived on the scene. Protestors shut down the Fourth Precinct in response. In 2016, Philando Castile was shot in a St. Paul suburb during a routine traffic stop after informing the officer he was carrying a licensed firearm. There was Terrance Franklin, who in 2013 was shot after a group of cops alleged he tried to grab one of their guns (a claim that Franklin's family vigorously disputes). Back in 2010, the MPD was involved in the death of David Smith, a mentally ill Black man who did not survive a confrontation in which he was tased and then held face down on the floor for several long minutes, a knee held firmly on his back long after he ceased being responsive.

Just like George Floyd.

I didn't think I would have any part to play in the George Floyd drama. I figured there would be protests, the department might call in a SWAT team, and that would more or less be it. I was a school resource officer, a guy who worked on campus. It was May 2020, and North High was in session, but because of the COVID-19 pandemic, learning was entirely remote. A number of schools were being used as sites for students to pick up breakfasts and lunches, and us SROs had been assigned to bounce back and forth between them, providing security. If that sounds excessive, it was actually in response to an incident that occurred the very first day we handed out meals, when a group of guys walked onto a school bus being used to transport food and took the driver's wallet. (We caught them the following day.) Even as things began to spiral after the George Floyd video exploded, I figured it'd remain business as usual for SROs.

I've never been so fucking wrong.

The next day, a Tuesday, I was put on standby in case of civic unrest. School resource officers spent the morning making our regular rounds, riot gear stowed in our car trunks just in case, after which we were to report to the Minneapolis Public Schools bus garage at 2 p.m. I was familiar with the spot—it's where we SROs gassed up our unmarked cars. At the appointed hour, ten of the city's fourteen SROs—the ones who had not already reported to the SWAT unit—were parked and waiting. And waiting. And waiting.

Meanwhile, the city went crazy.

It was in that parking lot that I first saw video, on my phone, of people breaking into the Target on Lake Street, which marked the beginning of the looting. It would only get worse. After a few hours, we finally received orders to head to the special operations center, the SOC, at Forty-First and Dupont, to pick up squad cars. If you'd have asked me earlier in the day, having something to do—anything to do—would have been preferable to sitting in that parking lot for another hour, but by that point information was rolling in, and now I wasn't so sure. The vandalized Target was directly across the street from Third Precinct headquarters, and not only had police been unable or unwilling to stop it, but rioters quickly shifted their focus to the station itself. Rather than have officers attempt to defend their territory and risk mass violence, the decision was made to simply vacate the premises. Everybody in the precinct—every officer, every investigator, every civilian employee—grabbed whatever they could and just split, relocating to the SOC. I saw them when I showed up to collect my squad car, and they were pissed. "Apparently, the chief and the mayor said it's just a building, so they can have it," one of the officers told me. "They don't want to jeopardize our safety."

Despite those orders, somebody made the decision to go back and fight for their turf. All kinds of weapons and ammunition were locked up in that building, not to mention offices filled with files and evidence. Off-duty officers still had uniforms and personal possessions in their lockers. I don't know how many cops returned after the building was vacated, but going against orders like that was stupid on many levels. They ended up trapped, the crowd swarming the building and blocking their exit. Then somebody set the place on fire and the cops inside had to be rescued by a SWAT team. The department was burning from the outside in and from the inside out. Third Precinct headquarters was destroyed.

We were ordered back to the bus garage, where I kept thinking about the concept of control. As police officers, we're taught to command whatever situation we might find ourselves in, by force if necessary. Maintaining control is the number one priority for an officer. Now, as a department, we were attempting to subdue the entire city of Minneapolis . . . and we were losing. Ceding that precinct building to an angry mob was a clear sign we'd lost control, and a giant signal flare that people were more or less free to do as they pleased around the city. The Third Precinct was on fire. The Target across the street had been virtually emptied by looters. Soon, grocery stores, restaurants, and so many other businesses—three hundred along Lake Street alone—were damaged, some irrevocably. A year later, one-third of them hadn't reopened. The final tally from those riots showed more than 150 cases of arson across the Twin Cities, contributing to more than $500 million worth of destruction. Fires were everywhere. Me and my fellow SROs watched it unfold on the news and social media while we waited for instruction.

The only thing already on my agenda was a 3 p.m. Zoom call with my football players, which was part of our regular pandemic schedule since we couldn't meet in person. To that point, I'd used our time together mostly just to check in on my guys. I viewed those meetings as vital to maintaining contact, and unless I was in the middle of a goddamn riot I wasn't about to miss it. Knowing that I was about to be inserted into the city's madness in some unforeseen way, I contacted my assistant coaches to make sure everybody logged on.

I was in the parking lot, standing amid school buses and gas pumps, when I joined the call. I got right to the point. "This might be the most important meeting I've ever held with you guys," I said. "It's going to be bad out there tonight, and I want all of you to stay home, far away from the action. I'm probably going to be in the heart of it, and I don't know how things will go. It might get really bad for the police. I'm not saying this is goodbye, but I want you all to know I love you. Now stay away, and handle your business wherever you are."

I was scared, but I'm good at putting up a stoic front. I did not want to panic the kids. Maintaining that calm, even if I wasn't feeling it, helped me settle down.

I wish I could say otherwise, but not everybody listened. Some of my players went out. Some of them looted. One even got caught with a carload of stuff, which I know about only because the player's mother told me later. There was so much chaos and crime in the city that night I don't think the police even detained him. They just confiscated the loot. (I might have disciplined him if I'd had the chance, but the kid didn't play that season for reasons unrelated to the riots.)

At 4 p.m. the ten SROs not already on SWAT details were instructed to report to the fire station in the Third Precinct. It was more comfortable than the bus garage, with couches and recliners, but I found it difficult to relax. We were in the dark about whatever lay ahead, but I knew it wouldn't be good. Our assignment was to protect the firefighters, and when the alarm bell finally sounded, it marked the end of anything approaching normal in my life until the following day. We set out to save a pawnshop that was ablaze on Twenty-Eighth and Lake.

Hearing where we were headed gave me pause. Isn't that in the middle of the riots? Shit. Of course that's where we were going. Those firefighters sure as hell needed an escort, but it didn't make sense to me why SROs were the ones chosen. Wouldn't a

SWAT team be better suited, or even patrol cops? It's not like everybody on the force saw action that night—plenty of active-duty officers stayed home. To ask a handful of school resource officers to gear up and march into the teeth of a riot seemed odd. It was like they skipped over everybody else and somehow landed directly on us.

We rolled with a handful of black-and-whites and a couple unmarked vehicles. I was in a squad car with Tyler Edwards, the SRO from Southwest High School, who I'd known for years through his help with the Brain and Body summertime kids' program. Back then, our SRO uniform was shorts and T-shirts; now it included Kevlar, helmets, and riot shields. As we followed the fire trucks down Lake Street, it seemed like every building was dark, the electricity cut off. Explosions rang out on all sides, blowing the night to pieces. Some of the bangs were only fireworks, totally harmless save for their impact on our nerves, but others were goddamn Molotov cocktails. Tyler kept the sirens quiet, wanting to attract as little attention as possible. It didn't help. As we navigated the streets, people pelted our vehicles with bottles, soup cans, and rocks. Each impact resounded with a terrifying boom inside the car. That trip became one long shudder. It was only beginning.

When the fire finally came into view, I could barely see it through the torrent of black smoke pouring from its center. The farther we drove, the blacker things grew. It was like the neighborhood had been dropped into a giant smokestack belching the densest, foulest pollution possible. It was dusk by that point, still plenty of daylight under ordinary circumstances, but we couldn't tell left from right, front from back, and soon we even lost sight of the fire itself. We were blind and stranded, separated from our support vehicles. Driving inches at a time, we finally made out an illuminated fire truck and homed in on that thing like moths to a porch light. As it turned out, so did the rioters. The firefighters and a handful of officers had already advanced toward the pawnshop, so Tyler and I were left to protect the perimeter, even though I didn't even know what we were protecting it against, where the perimeter actually was, or whether as the only cops in sight we would stand a chance against whatever was gathering out there in the dark.

We secured our gas masks and got out of the car to assess the situation. I had never gripped my baton more tightly. Gunshots sounded almost as soon as my foot hit the asphalt, but amid the chaos it was impossible to identify where they came from, or if they were even aimed at us. It might have been the end of the shooting, or just the beginning. Ten SROs were on that detail, somewhere, every one of us a sitting duck. Our only communication was the radio, but with our gas masks on it wasn't too effective.

I slowly made out people advancing on us, yelling things like "The only good cop is a dead cop!" When they got close enough to see that Tyler and I were both African American, they accused us of being traitors and Uncle Toms. I began to wonder whether I was in the right profession. How did these people not understand that we were there to help? I was hoping that my presence as a Black officer might calm things down, but that wasn't the case at all. The uniform was the uniform, and that's all that mattered to them.

The group quickly grew, and with that growth came fresh waves of anger. I'd hoped that people wouldn't want to hurt us because we were accompanying the fire department, and everybody loves a firefighter. Not that night. People were emboldened, throwing rocks, frozen water bottles, and anything else within reach. I even got hit by a carton of milk. So much was happening at once that it became impossible to focus on a single area of danger, which would mean discounting a host of others. Tyler and I ended up doing a slow pirouette on that corner, not turning our backs to any one direction for more than a few seconds at a time. I actually found myself comforted by the thought that every second I wasn't shot was one less second I had to make it through the night.

Even people who weren't actively violent took turns trying to antagonize us into an extreme reaction, mostly by squirting us with water. It was pure bait. Dozens of people were recording everything that happened. I knew I had to have thick skin, but I also knew that I can only be somebody's motherfucker for so long. That's a trigger word for me, and usually all it takes is one to set me off. Well, I must have absorbed a hundred motherfuckers that night, and I managed to keep my hands to myself. Being outnumbered ten to several thousand will have that effect.

The objects people threw grew bigger and bigger, including rocks large enough to chip the asphalt. The impacts sounded like gunshots. Some of them might have been gunshots. There were so many sounds, coming from everywhere at once. We can't do this by ourselves, I thought. As those rocks got closer and that group grew larger, we retreated a few steps at a time, hopeful that we were inching closer to the other SROs, wherever they were. Really, there was nowhere to go; we couldn't leave the rig, because that's what we were there to protect. It was the only moment in my entire career where I truly feared I would not make it home alive.

The longer we held our ground, the crazier it seemed that we were trying to protect firefighters who were working to save a neighborhood whose residents didn't seem to care whether or not it burned to the ground. If those folks wanted us to leave, that was fine by me. What were we even doing there? Was I helping? Was any of this helping? I sure hoped so. Short of having to intervene if somebody actually attacked a firefighter, my main job was to serve as a presence. And a target.

Tyler and I were hypervigilant about who or what constituted the most immediate threat at any given moment, and I ran through nonstop scenarios about what to do if somebody—or everybody—came at us. Where are my guys? Even if we were all together we didn't have nearly the numbers for effective crowd control, and I couldn't locate a single colleague. Finally, mercifully, the wind shifted, and I made out some people in blue through the smoke. There was my lieutenant. There were a couple of cops in a parking lot. We gathered together and held that perimeter until the fire was out . . . at which point we could not return to the fire station fast enough. The return ride passed mostly in silence, Tyler and I both too shell-shocked to speak.

At the firehouse I removed my vest and helmet like a guy fresh home from work loosening his tie and kicking off his shoes. I sunk deep into one of the couches, mission accomplished. As far as I was concerned, our work for the night was done. Little did I know.

Before long, we received a call about a fire at the Hi-Lake Shopping Center, only a few blocks away. Those were significant blocks.

It was close to midnight. Tyler drove. Back at the pawn-shop, he hadn't wanted to turn on the sirens. Now he didn't even want to turn on the headlights. The streets were mobbed and overflowing. At one point, Tyler, ever the optimist, rolled down his window to ask folks to get out of the way. "Roll that shit up, *now!*" I yelled, which he did, just before a gigantic loogie smacked against it, followed immediately by a random hard object. We couldn't take liberties like talking to people. Nothing fucking mattered; it was chaos.

Hi-Lake was an L-shaped strip mall with a parking lot in the middle and a standalone apartment building off on one side. Flames shot out from shops in the far corner, and before we knew it, an auto parts store was also on fire. Then a clothing store. If our first fire had been defined by smoke, this one was all about flames. Even from our position behind the fire rigs the heat was overwhelming.

Things grew scary as soon as we left the car. Hell, they were already scary. They got scar*ier*. I thought there were a lot of people at our first fire, but these numbers dwarfed those. Rioters quickly surrounded us. People wielded baseball bats and traffic signs—stop signs, no-parking signs, still on their posts—as weapons. Rocks flew from every direction. These folks weren't there to cuss us out, but to injure us, and their numbers were too large to handle. My radio crackled with my supervising sergeant making multiple, desperate calls for reinforcements. Crickets. There were nine hundred cops in the city—how in the fuck are only ten SROs on this detail?

As if the scene wasn't terrifying enough, our vantage on the corner put the Third Precinct into clear view . . . and it was still on fucking fire. Oh yeah, that. If they couldn't prevent people from destroying a police station, we didn't have much hope for backup.

We held our ground for an hour, maybe two—things are such a blur that it's impossible to recall. It seemed like every moment flip-flopped between our own aggression in trying to hold back the throng and the crowd's aggression in releasing some deep-seated civic frustration on us. I never thought my body armor and riot shield could feel so ineffective, but I might as well have been holding up a trash can lid. I tossed a steady stream of complaints Tyler's way. "This is not good." "It's bullshit that we're the only ones here." "Man, we shouldn't be here."

"We have to go." "We *really* have to go!" I kept saying that last one mostly because I knew we *couldn't* go, that our whole reason for being at that mall was to stay exactly where we were. That made me angry. The rising flames incited the mob, which grew increasingly antagonistic and progressively more violent with each passing minute. For me, the final factor was that our only way in or out—the two street entrances to the parking lot—would soon be completely blocked by people, the massing crowd clogging every avenue of escape. At that point it became an issue of preserving our own lives versus preserving other people's property. I didn't know whether there were people inside the nearby apartment building, or if it was in danger of catching fire. Maybe it was already on fire. Under ordinary circumstances that would have been a priority, but in that spot, at that time, we had no leeway. The firefighters hadn't quite extinguished the flames from the main structure, but they'd tamped them down. We hoped it would be enough because I wasn't joking when I said we had to go.

"We need to get the fuck out of here," I shouted at the lieutenant. "We're outnumbered, and it's dangerous." I'd reached the point where I didn't give two shits about the chain of command. It's not like I was spilling secrets—the lieutenant had been thinking the same thing. He made sure the firefighters were on board with the plan, rounded up the officers, and we beat a retreat back to the firehouse.

It wouldn't last. I *knew* it wouldn't last. Removing ourselves from immediate danger was just a setup for orders sending us to a different threat . . . or, as it happened, to the same threat as before. Those strip mall flames didn't continue to die down as we'd hoped. Without attention, they reignited and again threatened to spread. Within an hour, we were ordered back to the front line, to the same spot we'd just vacated. Our mission was clear, and so was the risk. Ultimately, we had no choice, so we went.

Any hope I had that the crowd might have settled down in the intervening time was shattered as soon as we pulled up. Somehow there were even more people than before. We passed a couple of our unmarked vehicles en route, abandoned by officers in favor of clearer paths to safety. The cars had been beaten into dented masses, their windows broken out from front to back.

All those people in the parking lot presented a logistical hurdle when it came to reaching the fire. The closest hydrant was about a hundred yards from the flames, and, with their trucks unable to breach the masses, the firefighters unfurled a long hose to reach it. That hadn't been an issue the first time around, when most of the rioters were on the other side of the lot. Now, though, that hydrant needed protecting. Water flow could not be interrupted. Tyler and I were assigned sentry duty, alone on an island. If there was a bright side, fewer objects seemed to be landing around us. Maybe people had run out of things to throw.

Our saving grace, if you can call it that, arrived at about 3 a.m., when the National Guard rolled in with Humvees and long guns. When they showed up, everything parted like the

Red Sea. Those guys offered the first sense of relief I'd felt all night. That was pretty much the end of this particular riot; as soon as the string of armored vehicles arrived, everybody on the street more or less took off. I guess that's the difference between the batons and riot shields of the police and the semi-automatic rifles of the National Guard. After that, getting the fire under control seemed easy. Within an hour it was done. So was I.

It must have been 4:30 a.m. when I got home. My wife and kids were still up. They'd been watching the news all night long. I'd like to talk about our tearful reunion and how I was mobbed in the entry hall, but it was hardly that dramatic. We'd been exchanging texts all night long, them consistently asking if I was okay and me consistently trying to dodge the truth. At no point before I got off duty did I have any idea of how okay I actually was, but I was at least in good enough shape to text back. It wasn't until I walked in the door and my family said I smelled like barbecue—the result of all the smoke I'd absorbed—that they began to realize exactly how deep in it I'd been.

At that point all I wanted to do was collapse into bed. I hit that pillow and slept for the next ten hours.

The following day I received instructions to report to the armory, where the department stored its weapons. After the Third Precinct burned, police brass wanted to take no chances with anyplace else. I handled the overnight shift for the next few days and didn't hear a peep from the rioters.

For once, some news involving the MPD that made me happy.

Could we have seen this kind of thing coming? Hell yeah, we could've. When people ask me about Derek Chauvin, I tell them, "What you saw in that video is 100 percent a case of 'Shut the fuck up because I'm in charge.'" Everybody in America saw it. Chauvin is the kind of guy who, the more you tell him what to do, he'll do the opposite just to prove he's in control. I think he stayed on George Floyd's neck because getting up would have seemed like he was taking instructions from everybody around him. It's easy to picture him saying, "Fuck that. I'll stay right the hell where I am."

The control issue is one we as police officers face every day. A couple of years earlier at North High, I encountered an incident of my own, from the opposite direction. I was on the sidewalk shortly after dismissal, making sure no outsiders hung around as kids loaded onto their buses. As the SRO, I made it known that if you weren't a North High student, you had to be at least two blocks away from campus when school got out. Hang out all you want, just don't do it in front of my school. Everybody knew that rule. I stood on that corner every day.

That's where I was when a police call went out about a group of teenagers passing a gun around in an alley so close to campus that I could see one end of it from where I stood. A minute later, four kids emerged. I made them out immediately and watched as they approached the school. When they got close enough, I drew my gun and shouted, "Get to the ground, NOW!" Thankfully, they complied.

They were all high school students, though none of them went to North. I kept them face down on the cement while I waited for backup. As rumors raced through the neighborhood about a cop holding a bunch of teenagers at gunpoint, people came out of the woodwork. A group of local peacekeepers began peppering me with comments like, "These kids were just walking by, minding their own business." Onlookers made a bunch of noise about how they were recording everything on their phones. "Just hold tight," I told them. "You've gotta give me some space." I ordered the crowd to back up.

When other officers arrived, one of them covered the suspects while I felt their pockets. It turned out they *all* had guns. Toy guns. A local gang called the SUB Stickup Boys had made recent practice of robbing people with fake guns. I didn't know if that's what this was, but until I figured it out I was going to treat them as if they were real. Meanwhile, a lady stormed up, shouting at top volume about how we were messing with people for no reason. Well, she hadn't heard the radio call that went out, and she hadn't seen the guns I'd found. The part that really got to me was that the cop who was covering the boys while I searched them didn't know those guns were fake, and he *still* turned around and tried to explain things to her. "See," he started saying, "we got a call . . ."

I cut him off. No, we didn't get a call. We got a *gun* call. We have four guys on the ground right here, and they *all* have guns. This guy is going to turn his attention away from armed suspects to convince a passerby that, no ma'am, we are not just messing with the citizenry? I about lost my mind. "Don't do that!" I yelled. "You don't have to explain anything to her until we have this situation under control."

There's that word again. *Control.*

That incident gave me perspective. Well-meaning people end up jeopardizing officer safety all the time because of their perception of law enforcement. Well, not every cop out there is racist. As a Black officer, I could probably get away with hemming up some Black kids and getting a little bit physical. Even if I was blamed for overreach, nobody's going to accuse me of racism. That cop who was covering the boys, though, was white. Maybe it's why he was more worried about people's perceptions than with his own safety, or mine. As a result, he failed to maintain control. It didn't cost us, but it easily could have.

That explains part of the George Floyd situation. As it happened, one of the people on the video telling Chauvin to get up off of George's neck—the guy wearing a hoodie with Northside Boxing Club written on it—helped coach wrestling at North High. His name is Donald Williams, and I know him pretty well. Donald was absolutely doing the right thing in standing up for George, but given this particular circumstance, I can't help but wonder whether, had not spoken up—if every bystander on that street corner had just kept quiet—Chauvin, with nothing to prove, might have relented on his own. It's a fucked-up way to think, but that's the reality of the Minneapolis Police Department, where a massive majority of officers feel that citizens, especially those in the poorer neighborhoods, owe *us*. I know this because I worked there for twenty years. In places with gangbangers and high crime rates, cops think that people should feel lucky we're around. It's true to a degree, but it's also the opposite of protect and serve. And it's the root of every riot we saw that fateful night.

The underlying message from those anti-police crowds, whether speaking peaceably in city council meetings or shouting over bullhorns as part of mass gatherings, is that they're tired of being treated like criminals without having done anything wrong. We are citizens of this city and of this country, so deal with us appropriately. Do not treat victims like suspects. These are not difficult concepts to grasp.

Some officers, though, swing in precisely the opposite direction. George Floyd was sitting in his car when the police showed up, called on suspicion he'd passed a counterfeit $20 bill. Given that he was entirely passive, was that kind of police response necessary? Hell no, it wasn't.

To me, it's important to note that these details speak more of a toxic workplace than institutional racism. There are some racists in the MPD, of course, just as I'd imagine there are racists on every police force in the country. There are also some assholes—more than a few, in fact—whose bad behavior transcends their interpretation of race. Derek Chauvin was one of them. I knew the guy personally, and while I thought he was aloof and awkward at first, and a fucking jerk based on what he did to George Floyd, I have no clue whether he's actually racist. I'll give him this much, though: what I saw on that video speaks to many broken parts of his personality, but racism isn't one of them. In a police department made up of 88 percent whites, it's easy to look at white cops working Black neighborhoods and attribute any questionable action to bigotry. The way I see it, it's mostly bad training.

It is drilled into police officers to be wary of people at all times in all circumstances. It is vital to our own self-preservation. You never know who's armed, and you never know who, during a routine encounter, might be willing to spill your blood. So you keep everybody at arm's length. We deal with people at their worst moments—strung out, injured, victimized, and frequently bent on deceiving us. Until a police officer can figure out who's who in a potentially dangerous situation, we have to assume the worst. When I said I wonder whether George Floyd might still be alive if bystanders hadn't urged Chauvin to get off of his neck, it wasn't just a wishful notion. Speaking from my own experience as a police officer, when a random outsider tried to tell me how to do my job while I was in the middle of *doing* my job, I tended to have a similar response. I sure hope I have better sense than Derek Chauvin about these kinds of things, but if you had tried to tell me my business before I'd fully secured a scene, you probably wouldn't have liked my response.

Part of that is hardwired into me. I had a field training officer who dinged me for needing instruction to do simple things that I was about to do anyway. He once gave me a bad score because he told me to fasten my seatbelt as I was in the process of reaching for my seatbelt. I compared it to him approaching me at a stall in the men's room and saying, "Don't forget to urinate." I was literally *right there*. It's a trivial example, but it's a sign of the control our police environment demands from the beginning of one's career to the end. It's an exhibition of power, passed from one generation to the next.

The entire George Floyd encounter was textbook police work up to Chauvin's knee on his neck—including drawing the gun, ordering George out of the car, let me see your hands, all of that. I did those things a million times, and if I had been in charge of the Floyd situation I'd probably have followed that pattern. It was only after George had clearly been subdued that things went sideways. One thing I never heard discussed publicly is that, when a person the size of George Floyd has his hands cuffed behind his back, it's almost impossible for him to get up from the ground without assistance, even from a sitting position. Everybody in law enforcement knows that. The entire thing could have been handled without incident if the moment George complained about not feeling right Chauvin declared it a medical situation, ceased touching him at all, and instructed him to sit and wait until an ambulance arrived. Doing anything else showed us what kind of man Derek Chauvin really is.

I've heard people say that the other cops on the scene didn't do enough to stop Chauvin, but in my mind their response goes hand in hand with their training. Two of those cops, Tom Lane and James Keung, were recent hires. Most of Keung's field training to that point had come under Chauvin. They'd arrived on the scene first; Chauvin showed up later and assumed control. What were those guys supposed to do? You were recently my FTO, and now I'm supposed to tell you, after only a week on the force, how to do your job? Officers aren't afforded the leeway to push back against one of their own, especially with a power imbalance in play. Lane and Keung didn't understand that they had a choice, a voice. That's not their fault. It's the culture.

Let's also be clear about what field training is and what it's intended to do. Field training is not set up for officers to succeed, it's designed to weed out unfit cops—recruits that trainers think won't make it. If you struggle in a given area of police work, you will likely receive little or no guidance on how to improve. The police manual includes few standards about how things should be done. Because community service officers in Minneapolis go through five training periods, they frequently encounter conflicting instructions on how to execute a given directive, and then they have to learn an entirely new way of doing things once they join the force and report to a superior. It's all about power, and sometimes it gets personal. I experienced it myself while in field training: because I did not want to pull over cars with busted taillights, my FTO branded me a bad cop. At that point, creating quality police officers is no longer the primary goal. Chauvin had at least seventeen misconduct complaints on his record, yet he was still training recruits.

It's a system with no process to measure improvement, or even to provide much feedback. Tom Lane might have wanted to avoid being on a call with Derek Chauvin ever again, but he had no avenue to communicate that. I actually knew Tom quite well before the George Floyd incident. Before he joined the force, he'd volunteered for my summertime Brain and Body camp, helping us run activities and chaperone events. As I knew him, Tom was a great guy. Every kid in the program loved him, partly because he was so nice and partly because he was a pushover. I tended to keep the locations of upcoming outings a secret, to prevent kids from picking and choosing when they attended. Those kids were smart enough to recognize a mark, though, and consistently tricked Tom into spilling the beans. This is a compliment, not a criticism; Tom was trying to connect with kids and make them comfortable, and that's exactly what he did.

In the aftermath of the riots, MPD chief Medaria Arradondo went on TV and said that silence from the three officers alongside Chauvin equaled complicity, which would be an amazing standard if it was actually true. Let's be clear, though—in the minutes before George Floyd died, Tom did not have the institutional power, either actual or implied, to order Chauvin to cease and desist. Once George lost consciousness, Tom strongly suggested that Chauvin turn him onto his side, and Chauvin refused. Had Tom upended the chain of command and physically intervened, he probably would have been dog-walked—that's cop talk for "treated like shit"—through the entire department. If he'd pushed Chauvin off of Floyd, allowing that incident to end in a nondescript way, nobody would have assumed a life had been saved. Instead, people inside the department would have ridiculed Tom for superseding police hierarchy. Sergeants and lieutenants wouldn't have wanted him on their shifts. He'd have encountered trust issues at every level. It's impossible to say any of this with certainty, but had Tom intervened, my guess is that he'd have effectively been drummed off the force. He ended up with a thirty-month federal prison sentence for his part in the incident. Keung got thirty-six months of federal time, and another officer, Tou Thao, who kept bystanders away while the other three restrained George, got forty-two months. (All three also collected state charges.) Chauvin got twenty-one years.

After almost every officer-involved shooting, talk within the station focuses on justifying whatever the police did, no matter how things actually went down. It's basically a self-supporting culture because the officers doing the talking may end up in a similar situation themselves one day. It took George Floyd's death for cops to admit just how fucked up things can get and how easily events could have ended differently. Even then, I heard more than a few officers talking about how if Floyd had done this or hadn't done that—had he somehow responded differently as a victim—he'd still be alive today. I don't know if they were trying to condone Chauvin's actions, but it sure sounded like it to me.

Breaking it down further, when it came to George Floyd, the justification I encountered from white cops was different than it was from Black cops. Way different. Anytime I heard somebody harping on George for not behaving differently at the outset, that was a white cop talking. Every Black cop I spoke with understood that George was subdued *before* Chauvin did his thing. Pinning him down when he was already immobilized made no sense.

Why can Black cops see what white cops can't? I'm speaking in generalities here, not about any specific officer, but the answer is simple: in the eyes of many white cops, Black men present an increased threat. Black cops recognize the foolishness of that proposition because we know how we're looked at by the outside world when we don't have our uniform on. I think about the time my SUV broke down in a Target parking lot near closing time, and I had to wait for a tow truck. Soon, mine was the only vehicle remaining, and it must have looked to employees like I was casing the place. They called the police, and the guy who showed up automatically approached me with suspicion—another case of a citizen in need treated like a suspect. As soon as I flashed my badge, everything changed. Suddenly he was as nice as could be, there to protect, not to prosecute. He asked what he might do to help. I can only wonder how that incident might have ended had I been in any other line of work.

I've even had that kind of thing happen to me inside a police station. Early in my career, I arrived in civilian clothes for my shift at the Third Precinct because all my gear was in a locker downstairs. Three cops were minding the door. "This is an officers' entrance," one of them said.

"Yeah, I know," I replied. I didn't feel like explaining myself.

"So who are you?" one of them said.

I stopped and faced them. "I'm Charles Adams," I said. "I work mid-watch. You think I'd fuckin' walk through the employee entrance of a police station if I wasn't supposed to be here?" Those guys' job is to guard the gate; it's on them to know who's supposed to be coming and going. I couldn't help but wonder if they'd have held up a white man in a similar fashion.

Put on that uniform, though, and it's all different. That's one thing Black officers understand implicitly.

After the riots finally cooled down, community reaction against the MPD was swift and visceral. Taking public grief for wearing the uniform was one thing, but entire institutions began to cut ties. Organizations from the Minneapolis Parks and Recreation Board to the Minneapolis Institute of Art to the Minnesota Orchestra stopped using off-duty MPD officers for event security. The University of Minnesota dramatically scaled back its relationship with the force.

Pertinent to me, the Minneapolis Public School board voted unanimously to terminate the MPD's contract for providing school resource officers on campuses. That's when I learned that the board members and I do not share the same values. Despite police having worked with the school district for nearly fifty years, during the meeting at which the decision was reached, one board member said that "it is completely unnatural to have police in schools." The board labeled our presence traumatic for students and said money dedicated to us could be better spent. Those claims might be true for some school districts, and even for some schools within our own district, but at North High, the SRO position was vital long before I came on board, and that need never changed. In a neighborhood as violent as ours, having a sworn officer on hand to protect a vulnerable population from outside threats and to serve as a link between the community and the police paid dividends every single day. Minneapolis's entire SRO roster had been interviewed and hand selected from MPD ranks by the school board's office of emergency management, safety, and security. We were qualified, and we were really good at our jobs.

Notably coming to the MPD's defense at that school board meeting was a cadre of North High students and their families, rallying in support of the program, and of me personally. One kid said I was "like a father" to him. "With SROs being gone," said another, "nobody's going to feel safe at school." A board member offered an amendment to allow North and Patrick Henry, the city's two poorest high schools, both of which are in my neighborhood, to keep their SROs. It did not pass. The thinking was that when police are needed, the school can just call 911. What was lost with that decision is a personal connection between the police department and every school in the district. Administrators can hardly expect that a random squad car responding to a call will possess the kind of knowledge necessary to handle a given situation in a way that best suits the environment. Hell, it took me several weeks on the job to realize I couldn't treat these kids like I would ordinary suspects.

This idea was laid out by the Justice Department in a June 2023 report that utterly trashes the MPD. I'll get into the meat of those findings later; pertinent to this topic are multiple details of officer interactions with youths in which the cop failed to use age-appropriate de-escalation—or any de-escalation at all. Why is this important? The report gives us that information, too, and none of it comes as a surprise. Adolescents, it says, are more impulsive than adults and less able to exercise judgment. "In the stress of a police encounter," the report reads, "youth may have difficulty thinking through the consequences of their actions and controlling their responses." Can that lead to unnecessary confrontations with officers? You bet your ass it can. For an officer with relevant experience, however, de-escalation is second nature. Unfortunately, those of us with the most experience in that regard have all been shuffled away from the schools.

Now, not only were our schools without a police presence, but the entire system was without the Brain and Body summer program I'd launched, which died along with the MPD's school contract. It had been run entirely by school resource officers during summer vacation, and with everybody back on regular patrol there was no way to keep it going. In fact, a city council member called me shortly after that school board vote, asking what was needed to further support Brain and Body. Nothing, I told him—with the cops who ran it now on other assignments, there was nothing left to support. "You got rid of everybody," I said sadly. "Before you guys make rash decisions, you should probably do better research."

Brain and Body wasn't the only casualty of the board's decision. Our community engagement unit and the Police Activities League—which, like the SRO program, were staffed by on-duty officers—were also disbanded. Just like that, our ability to connect with the people we served, along with all our youth programming, was effectively disabled.

Especially maddening for me was that the people decrying the police department's relationship with the schools were not the people whose kids attended those schools. They were wealthy white folks in South Minneapolis who were convinced they knew what was best for Black kids in our Northside community. With no basis of understanding, they said that kids in our schools were already suffering and would be triggered by cops in the building. It's easy to claim you don't need police in your life when you live in a violence-free neighborhood. How would it look for a Northsider like me to tell those guys what's best for their schools? I don't know because I wouldn't even consider it. Their intentions were good, but shit were they shortsighted.

After the decision to let the SROs go, incidents in and near schools increased rapidly. It took less than a year for the principals of six Minneapolis high schools, including North, to release a statement addressing "increased levels of violent crime" and decrying "a lack of safety planning." "Continue to be vigilant, stay together, and avoid lingering," they wrote. With no MPD contract, they had to seek out community volunteers to help monitor things.

North High's principal, Mauri Friestleben—a strong proponent of the SRO system—added an addendum on the school's Facebook page, warning of "cars with unknown passengers, circling after school lets out and following and/or robbing students once they're a block or so away from school." Roosevelt High's principal wrote about muggings in the neighborhood and robberies of local businesses.

A year later, things hadn't much improved. In late 2022, a group of armed teenagers tried to break into multiple high schools during school hours, presumably to conduct assaults. They got inside the building at Edison before administrators managed to expel them. My dad and Rick Plunkett—police officers on my coaching staff—received early word and warned the North High administration just in time. The same group showed up at North and was met at the door by a beefed-up adult presence. They never made it in. I can't help but think that if those kids had intended indiscriminate violence, administrators would have had little chance of stopping them. An SRO on duty would have meant not only an armed police officer but direct radio contact with the precinct. Now a school representative has to call 911, a process with abundant shortcomings.

In October 2022, more than one hundred people gathered for a public forum in the North High School auditorium in which parents addressed local political leaders, including the mayor and the superintendent, about their fears of violence. Multiple teachers spoke about the difficulty of managing a classroom full of grieving children while they were deep in grief themselves—not just once, but again and again. One talked about how students don't feel safe at dismissal time. Another said that kids can barely walk around the campus, let alone beyond it. Police representatives were there, including my dad, though the only answers they could provide—increased patrols, promises to respond promptly to emergency calls—were a far cry from the thing that would help most: a full-time cop on school grounds. Just parking my unmarked white Chevy Malibu in the spot marked OA for me in the school lot was enough to deter potential criminals. When they saw that car, they knew I was around. During school hours I was *always* around.

My last day as an SRO actually occurred before the fact. Schools had been shut due to the pandemic when the decision came down, so my last duty on campus actually occurred a couple of months earlier, when everybody in the building was sent home with hopes of returning in a week or two. It didn't work out that way. I had no idea it would be my last day on the job. The next time I stepped foot on North High property I was the football coach and nothing more.

The other thing North High lost along with its SRO was my open office door. Kids came in throughout the day to discuss all kinds of issues. I knew many of them through football, but a number of other students showed up as well, to talk about home life, school troubles, and romance issues. I had discussions with a lot of boys about a lot of girls. They'd bring in their lunch and chat with me and each other, just kids having conversations. I made sure to always have extra chairs around. Even kids who came in to discuss football would inevitably open up about other topics. Frequently my football talks ended up not being about football at all.

When I think about what that office meant to students at North, my mind immediately goes to a kid I knew years ago. He was on the autism spectrum—high-functioning and able to handle his coursework, but with difficulty containing day-to-day frustrations. My office became his go-to place when he could not manage in the classroom. I set him up with his own desk and gave him a green light to come and go, no questions asked. I had his independent education plan altered to include my office as a meditation room whenever the stresses of school grew overwhelming. This boy came in literally every day, usually with his chest stuck out, acting angry. He'd head straight to his desk with little more than a nod and do his work until the bell rang. Then he'd head to his next class. Early on I gave him a pair of boxing gloves and brought him to the nearby weight room, where he could punch out his frustrations on the heavy bag. That became part of our routine. After breaking a sweat, he was usually able to return to class. We did that for years. Toward the end, his grandmother came in to see me. "I don't know what you're doing with him, but I love it," she said. "I don't think he talks too much in school, but when he comes home he can't stop talking about you." That was nice to hear, but I already knew how the boy felt. Grandma was right—the kid didn't verbalize much—but when you see somebody every single day, even unsaid things become clear.

If there's a current version of that student roaming the halls of North High, I don't know what kind of support he's getting. My office has been given to a social worker, so whatever football meetings I have—usually with colleges, promoting my players—take place in the equipment room.

I have one more example to illustrate the benefits of employing an SRO at North. It's purely conceptual, but it's about the most impactful thing I can conceive of. I believe that had I been on the job the day of the Amir Locke walkout in February 2022, Deshaun Hill might still be alive.

Please hear me: I don't blame D-Hill's death on anyone but the devil who shot him. Still, every time I envision Deshaun leaving campus that day, there's not a single scenario in which he avoids walking past me. I'd have been stationed right there at the front door, and when I saw Deshaun, we'd almost certainly have spoken. If he was looking for someplace to go or something to do apart from joining the march, I could have steered him to the weight room or even back to class. I can't say he would have listened, but knowing Deshaun, I believe he would have.

So what are the costs of removing SROs from Minneapolis public high schools? Start with the life of one of the best young men on campus. I don't need anything more than that when I say the school board should have known better.

Within hours of the school board vote, SROs were ordered to return our work vehicles within twenty-four hours and then report to the Third Precinct, relocated to the downtown convention center after the original headquarters burned. They had basically lost a shift's worth of officers to PTSD and assorted riot-related ailments, and we had to cover. Just like that, I found myself back on patrol duty for the first time in fourteen years.

I spent most of my working days answering 911 calls. One change since I'd last patrolled was that we were no longer allowed to ride by ourselves, in part because in the aftermath of the riots, people were actively trying to do us harm. One vacant hotel in South Minneapolis had been taken over by hundreds of squatters, including an anti-police faction that tried to lure cops inside with fake calls of medical distress. By the time I hit the streets, we were prohibited from going anywhere near the place. I must have received three or four calls to that location and, adhering to our new protocol, told them to meet me two blocks away. They never did.

Being back on the streets after so many years at North High was surreal. If there was a saving grace, it was that it took only about a week to have my reassignment request approved. That's how I found myself back home in the Fourth, the Northside. With Dad as precinct boss and my SRO position at North High School off the table, this was my next-best option.

That was a Wednesday. On Saturday, Chief Arradondo called me with a proposition. "The Vikings have asked for a meeting," he said. "They're reconsidering their relationship with the Minneapolis Police Department, and I'd like you to be there to represent us. That's what you'll do instead of patrol duty tomorrow."

In addition to being inspector of the Fourth Precinct, my father served as head of police security for the Vikings, in charge of off-duty assignments for officers working the stadium on game days. I'm not sure why they asked for me instead of him. Maybe it's that I was a prominent local football coach as well as a cop, and they figured I could relate to the players. I was all for it.

I can't say that the team's wavering commitment to the MPD came as much of a surprise. With fans barred from U.S. Bank Stadium during the pandemic, only eight officers had been retained during game days in case of emergency. Even that came with some controversy. Before the Vikings' season opener, the team staged a tribute to George Floyd featuring Alicia Keys and a video presentation. My dad, another officer, and I sat in the top row of the stadium's lower bowl to watch. We were caught on film as a local reporter panned around the stadium, and the clip went viral when somebody painted us in disrespectful tones, noting that we remained seated during the memorial. Never mind that we thought it was a great presentation, or that none of us even thought to stand while it played. It wasn't the national anthem.

The negative attention was enough for the Vikings to bring up the topic with my dad. To avoid further embarrassment, real or imagined, from that point on we were instructed to stay in the building's hallways during games, out of camera view. I'd been working Vikings games for decades, and sitting alone in a hallway, watching on TV, was not why I signed up. I worked only two or three more games then gave it up.

Now the team wanted to meet.

The session was held at a swank downtown social club used as headquarters by the sports management firm IFA, which represented a number of Vikings players. I was part of a police contingent that arrived in the same lounge area where I once attended Tyler Johnson's draft party to find maybe twenty Vikings players and assorted executives spread out on couches, chairs, and bar stools.

Vikings general manager Rick Spielman kicked things off, talking about why it was important for the team to address the issue of police participation after all that had happened. Given how many players showed up, including the team's entire leadership council, it was obvious that the players themselves were invested. Rick talked about concerns raised by the Vikings' continued relationship with the MPD and said it was only fair for them to hear our perspective before making a decision. He introduced Chief Arradondo, who explained the department's position on everything that had recently gone down, and detailed how he'd responded to it internally. He took some questions, and when one arose about the cops who worked games, he said, "OA, it might be good if you handle that one."

Yeah, it might.

I introduced myself and talked a bit about my history as a police officer and football coach. Then I got right to the point. "Can I talk to you here the way I talk on the field?" I asked. "Can I be me?"

Linebacker Anthony Barr piped up. "Go ahead, Coach," he said.

I held nothing back.

"Y'all motherfuckers gonna mess up my money, man," I said. "There's a lot of good brothers out here working games with me. If y'all want janky cops, or if y'all don't want cops who look like you, then get rid of the MPD and see what you end up with."

Now I had their attention. "If you get rid of MPD cops, you get rid of a lot of brothers who already work for you. We have solid guys here who do good, respectful work. My daddy runs it. If you take the MPD out of U.S. Bank Stadium, a lot of us won't be able to do that work anymore."

"We didn't know that," said linebacker Eric Kendricks.

I could tell this was the first time the players had considered the possibility of putting Black cops out of work. I think I'd just changed some minds. When the meeting ended, I was inundated with players wanting to talk. I passed out my phone number to a bunch of them. Spielman himself called me that night and asked me to advise his adult son, who was working on inner-city youth development. Needless to say, the Vikings maintained their relationship with the MPD. My dad heads police security for the stadium to this day.

I enjoyed fringe benefits from that meeting for a while. During a Zoom call with my players later that year, the Vikings' quarterback, Kirk Cousins, logged on. The kids were really into that. He took questions for a while, and after he signed off, all anybody wanted to talk about was how cool that had been. I gave the players a few minutes before trying to regain order, knowing full well what was coming up. No sooner had we resumed the meeting, a new Zoom box appeared. It was running back Dalvin Cook. "What's up y'all?" he said. My players about lost their minds. They were literally howling. Dalvin stayed on the line with us for about ten minutes and ended up offering $100 to anyone who could beat him in a push-up contest. Well, Polars running back Terrance Kamara, who went on to play for the University of Northern Iowa, accepted the challenge—and won. Dalvin sent the money to his cash app before the conversation even ended. By the end of the week the Vikings had sent a package of hoodies and goodies for our players. Seeing how thrilled my guys were by that Zoom meeting was in some ways even more satisfying than the NFL team's renewed commitment to the police department.

That wasn't the only thing to materialize in the aftermath. About two weeks after I met with the Vikings, the Twins called. They'd heard about what had gone down with their NFL neighbors and wanted a discussion of their own. Off-duty MPD officers also worked Twins games, but the team's position was the polar opposite of where the Vikings had been; instead of thinking about cutting ties, they wanted to know how they might better support us.

The same group of police representatives that had met with the Vikings showed up at a restaurant inside the Twins' downtown ballpark to address team executives, including owners Jim and Joe Pohlad, and manager Rocco Baldelli. They had some questions about police reform, including possible donations to the force through the ownership family's foundation. They also raised the topic of minority representation, which led directly to a dilemma they were facing with a statue located just outside the ballpark.

Former owner Calvin Griffith had moved the team from Washington, DC, to Minneapolis for the 1961 season, in the process changing its name from the Senators to the Twins. Griffith died in 1999, and the team commemorated him in bronze in 2010. Trouble was, Calvin Griffith was an unrepentant racist. Examples abound, none more prominent than when he was caught on tape at a speaking engagement in 1978. "I'll tell you when I came to Minnesota," he told the room. "It was when we found out there were only fifteen thousand Blacks here. Black people don't go to ball games but they'll fill up a wrestling ring and put up such a chant it'll scare you to death. We came here because you've got good, hardworking white people here."

That's fucked up in a hundred ways. Thankfully, the Twins seemed to realize it, too. During our meeting, the executives asked what I thought should be done with Griffith's statue. Honestly, I had no idea. I didn't even know the guy's history until they told me about it, but I said that if a statue makes people uncomfortable in the way *that* statue made people uncomfortable, I supported its removal.

When they asked about staffing, I gave different answers than I'd given the Vikings. I told them that for me, the Twins' police-staffing issues began and ended with a lack of diversity. A hundred cops were on twenty-five-man rotations to work Twins games at Target Field, and not one of them was Black. I'd continually asked for off-duty assignments at the ballpark over the years, but the lieutenant in charge of scheduling always had excuses for why he couldn't use me. "I would love the opportunity for myself and some other African Americans to work here as cops," I told the team brass. "It sure would say something about your emphasis on diversity."

As it turned out, they had a better idea. It took a few months before they told me what it was, but it was worth the wait. They made me a job offer. Our meeting was in June. That October, I accepted a position as the Twins' director of team security. It was the opportunity of a lifetime. I would accompany the ball club on road trips and ensure that safety protocols were met. I would travel with players from ballpark to hotel, hotel to airport, airport to ballpark, escort them to special events and signings, and become their executive protection. The position didn't offer much say over which cops were hired for ballpark security, but

I would at least be able to encourage minority officers to apply. I accepted the job.

In the meantime, a bunch of the cops who already worked for the Twins ended up quitting based on a rumor that Charles Adams was coming in and aiming for white cops' jobs. I guess they weren't willing to test the validity of such a ridiculous suggestion. Many of the cops who stuck around were guys who knew me personally and understood that that kind of maneuver isn't in my playbook . . . never mind that my new role involves team security, not ballpark security, and I couldn't affect their jobs even if I wanted to. Still, I managed to help four brothers land positions on the staff. It ain't much, but it's four more than they had before.

Also, they took down that Calvin Griffith statue.

Unlike my off-duty work with the Vikings, the role with the Twins was a full-time gig. Taking it meant I'd have to leave the force after twenty years—a decision that turned out to be less difficult than I anticipated. I canvassed opinions from my wife and my dad among many people, all of whom approved the transition. The paycheck was bigger, and turning it down would mean never knowing how I might be able to affect things from the inside. Making things easy was the knowledge that I could always return to law enforcement as long as I kept my license up-to-date.

Even with all that on the table, had the school board not cut ties with the MPD—if I was still an SRO, roaming the halls of North High like I used to do—I never would have left the force. That high school and that community are just too important to me. As it was, I issued a single demand before signing with the Twins: I'd give them whatever they needed, whenever they needed it, for most of the year. From June through November, though, my priority was the Polars. Any job I took had to carve out time for football practice and the ability to remain in Minnesota on game days, even if the Twins were on the road. They agreed.

It's easy to say that heading security for a major league baseball team is a dream come true, but the fact was, I already had my dream job: head football coach at North Community High School. And I wasn't about to give that up for anything.

Chapter 9

———

Reform

When I was in the academy, they asked us trainees to step into a gas chamber. Well, it was more like a trailer, designed to provide experience in tear gas situations. We had filtration masks, of course, but part of the drill required taking them off inside the trailer long enough to say your name, after which we could dart outside into the fresh air.

Well, department resources were limited, and they didn't have enough filters to go around. Given the liability involved with many of us being provided no protection, supervisors made the drill optional, at which point most of the cadets decided, cool, we'll just stay outside.

Then one of the lieutenants spoke up.

"I'm officially letting you all know that none of you has to do this," he said. "But if you opt out, I'll make sure you will never again get a requested shift."

We all went into that trailer, mask free.

I tell this story not as a complaint (honestly, being gassed like that was not as bad as I thought it would be), but as an illustration of how things work within a police department. A policy was enacted to protect cadets, which one possibly sadistic lieutenant decided mattered less than his own opinion about the situation. In a police department, that's how things frequently go.

Over my twenty years with the MPD, I had many thoughts about how to improve things. In his nearly forty years on the force, my dad has had even more. I've talked endlessly about it with him, with my uncle Tony, with my sister Brittney (who joined the force in 2021), and with countless colleagues. I have heard a *lot* of ideas about how things should look. There are no certainties when it comes to fixing what's wrong with the police, which is obvious because so many people have introduced so many ideas, and we're still having this conversation. The topic is especially tricky in Minneapolis.

Since 1961, Minneapolis's city charter has required 1.7 police officers per thousand residents, which today works out to a contingent of about 720. For a long time this was not an issue; in May 2020, the department employed about 900 officers. That's when George Floyd was killed and the rioting started. People have quit the force in droves ever since, succumbing to lingering PTSD or no longer able to tolerate how things are run. What's more, officers on regular retirement tracks are not being replaced in sufficient numbers because recruitment has all but dried up. As recently as 2015, the department received a thousand applications for employment. In 2019, that number was 292. Over the first ten months of 2022, fifty-seven people applied to be Minneapolis cops. Many were far from qualified, lacking either the requisite schooling or having red flags on their résumés. As of late 2022, the MPD roster was below 540—with only 260 of them on patrol—which was actually seen in some circles as good news, given that 90 percent of the department's budget goes to salaries, and budgets were being slashed up and down the line.

This reduction in force comes at a cost. Entire divisions, like procedural justice and our gang unit, have been wiped out. The MPD once had a racially diverse team of community response officers who handled things like warrants, drug busts, hot spots, and problem properties. Now they're extremely limited. Our officers can no longer work in the schools; many former SROs, like me, have left the department altogether. This is all happening amid a crime wave that is tearing apart neighborhoods like the Northside. Homicides have nearly doubled over the course of three years, with aggravated assaults increasing by a third. All the areas where cops were removed for lack of numbers are feeling the difference. Carjackings, robberies, gang shootings in broad daylight. We have more problem houses where gangbangers and drug dealers congregate because there are no resources to bust up those kinds of places. Things got so bad that residents actually sued the city for failing to maintain the charter-mandated officer numbers. The truth is there's not a lot we can do about it, at least in the short term. Nobody wants to be a cop.

Police departments across the country are feeling similar crunches and are taking all kinds of measures to increase hiring, including easing restrictions on things like marijuana use and tattoos, and reducing education requirements and physical ability tests. These adjustments might lead to more police, but will they lead to better policing?

It is a nuanced conversation. I keep thinking about that timed mile-and-a-half run I had to complete in order to graduate to the academy, and how being only a few seconds slower would have cost me my career. Careful consideration of the traits we want in recruits—and, importantly, what kinds of recruits we really ought to avoid—will benefit the department, especially as it pertains to its various litmus tests. I did a lot of good during my two decades with the MPD, and none of it might have happened because of a timed run at a distance that no cop ever has to make in the course of duty. When Dad took over the department's recruitment division in 2018, he asked around about that qualifying time. Where did it come from? How did the academy come up with that number? Nobody knew. When Dad thought about it, he realized that not only did it eliminate some otherwise promising officers, but it did so inequitably. For that requirement to be fair, it should include gender- and age-based considerations, like similar tests for the United States military. Mostly, Dad saw quality people in line to become quality cops being turned away from the force for reasons that made little sense and had virtually no bearing on what kind of police they would one day become. Dad got rid of that running test entirely. The MPD still has recruits run the distance, but now it's strictly for conditioning, not pass/fail.

They've even talked about doing away with drug tests. If that's what it takes to get more officers, I'm fine with it, though I will never accept an officer under the influence while on the job. The easy answer is to simply eliminate the drug test while maintaining restrictions for those convicted of drug crimes, and imposing strict consequences for those found to be using on duty.

One thing beyond the MPD's control is the requirement for a two-year college degree with a focus on policing. That's state-level policy, and is relatively unique—only a few departments around the country require anything beyond a high school education. Minnesota was the first to implement it, in 1978. As I see it, the original legislation was based largely on race, designed to prevent people of color from becoming cops. African Americans and women were just starting to apply for law enforcement jobs in noteworthy numbers, and this was a direct countermeasure, not intended in any way to make the organization more professional. Well, not only did we kick that barrier down, but I'd say we shattered it: the majority of Black officers in Minneapolis today have full four-year degrees, two years beyond the requirement. Many have a master's.

Even with its questionable origin, I think the two-year requirement is a good idea. I've seen what kind of difference it can make. Incoming officers must pass the Peace Officer

Standards and Training test, which is not easy. It's why I get so offended when people say our officers are not trained well. They must know the 609 and 385 codes by heart, and understand the elements of an array of crimes and juvenile justice statutes. The base of knowledge I picked up during my mandated college education allowed me to focus on actual policing once I joined the force, staying aware of my surroundings rather than trying to remember policies, procedures, and codes. There's also the idea that in earning a college degree, somebody accumulates not only knowledge but experience, having more interactions with a broader base of people. They possess a deeper understanding than whatever cultures they experienced in high school. The trouble with this idea is that in order to achieve "better" through standards that limit qualified applicants, you must sacrifice "bigger," and that equation isn't working out in the MPD's favor these days.

One thing people don't discuss much is that a lot of candidates are weeded out by human resources before the department even has a chance to consider them. In the winter of 2022, the department was looking for part-time investigators—nonsworn positions to help dig through a mountain of backlogged case files. Given that winter is my slow season with the Twins, I applied. They told me I was overqualified. I don't even know what that means. They needed help, and I am experienced in exactly the right ways. How does it make the department look if a twenty-year cop is willing to work cases part-time in his community and gets turned down while that position remains vacant? I have no answers.

Another policy Dad revisited during his time in charge of recruitment was background checks for prospective officers. The department had traditionally eliminated candidates for things like poor driving records, which have little bearing on one's potential and which can be corrected with training. In fact, my longest-tenured assistant football coach at North High, Rick Plunkett, had tried to become a police officer years earlier and was rejected because his license was suspended for an issue with child-support payments—which he'd hoped to resolve by embarking on a career as a police officer. He didn't get the job. After Dad took over, he eliminated that requirement. Rick joined the force and paid off his debt. And he's a damn good cop, if I say so myself.

I've long said that any reform of the police department must start with recruits. If new cops are learning the same things as the old ones, in the same way, how will anything change? Right now, the academy is run like the military, with sergeants wearing drill instructor hats and barking at trainees over trivial details, making them do push-ups for minor infractions. When you hear people talk about demilitarizing the police, this is part of what they're referring to, and it leads to some obvious questions. If we're preparing these officers for war, who is the enemy? Who are they fighting against? Usually, it's citizens in the community. How different could things be if, instead, we trained officers in concepts of collaboration and service?

That drill sergeant mentality might have worked better when my father came up because so many recruits were fresh out of college. These days, many prospective officers see policing as a career change. Thanks in part to the MPD's cadet program, which pays for the training of college-educated people who are considering a transition to police work, a higher percentage of recruits today are in their thirties and forties, have families, and many years of employment—yet they're still being treated like kids. Ultimately, when they hear enough academy instructors curse them out like they were boot camp privates, they begin to think that's how they're supposed to talk to people on the street. None of it is productive.

We need to show them how to do the job respectfully, with a model in which prospective officers learn to respond instead of react. Providing listening strategies might mean the difference between diffusing situations and inflaming them. That piece alone would have saved George Floyd, plus countless other citizens who have found themselves at the wrong end of police aggression. It's not a difficult premise, but many MPD trainers don't get it. They don't want to get it. They are stuck in a typical police mindset where they know best, and their power must be respected no matter what. What those old-school officers don't understand is that they have *more* power when they're able to ask for help from members of the community. That was my strength as a patrolman. I always wanted to know what was going on in the neighborhood. Jumping into a setting and immediately issuing orders is rarely productive. I tried to observe every situation, which included identifying who might help me figure things out. If people start jabbering, I try to keep it orderly. "Hold on, we'll get to the bottom of this, but first things first: Where's the person involved in the incident call? Let's start from there." I'd approach people I recognized and ask, "What did you see, what do you know?" The more people trust you, the more likely they'll be willing to talk. It's the art of conversation. At a crime scene, I don't want to assume anything. It's common sense. When recruits are militarized, trained to see everybody around them as a potential threat, that advantage disappears.

I remember an incident where a young man was shot while taking out his trash. When investigators went to the hospital to interview him, he was standoffish. "I ain't talking to none of y'all," he spat. There was only one cop he was willing to open up to: me. I'm not saying I was better than those officers, only that I'd spent so much time integrating myself into the Northside community that people knew I would treat them appropriately and respectfully. That is a benefit to working where you live. That kid never had an issue with trying to figure out who shot him, he just didn't trust opening up to a random officer because he didn't know how his information would be used. When I told him he was in good hands with those guys, that was all it took; the moment he trusted the system was the moment we made progress. People know I'll get the information where it needs to go, no questions asked.

That's only the beginning.

I've detailed my own problems with field training officers. Such problems were, and are, not unique to my experience. The word "training" is right there in their title, but many FTOs take it as their mission to treat their trainees like blank canvases, turning them into mini versions of themselves, even when their instructions have little bearing on what was taught at the academy. *Forget everything you learned and do things my way.* That's a common theme.

The qualifications for being an FTO mostly involve raising your hand when they ask for volunteers. A screening process helps, but they don't train the trainers. That leads back to my point about thinning the stock too aggressively because recruits are being let go for fixable things like inadequate report writing. Under the current system, you're expected to know something without being taught how to do it. As a football coach, I can't expect you to play quarterback if I don't give you the tools to be successful.

First, how does the way you write a report determine whether you'll be a good cop? Second, you need report-writing experience to write good reports. If your FTO dings you on that without helping you develop the necessary skills, that's pretty much all she wrote. You're done. To me, being an FTO should involve less of whatever the department refers to as "training," and more coaching.

In my sister's class, four or five people were released from duty the day before they were set to graduate. They made it all the way through, and then weren't even given a chance to work patrol. From a big-picture perspective, the specifics behind those decisions aren't important. The point is that you're down four or five cops during a time when staffing is at a premium. It makes no sense.

To my mind, civilians—actual teachers, not cops—should help train FTOs. Ideally, every officer on the force should go through that FTO training. Not only would it make them better officers, but whenever an FTO is absent during a shift—something that happens frequently—their recruit would be passed off to somebody qualified. Everybody wins.

I would get actual coaches—from the Twins, the Vikings, the University of Minnesota, or any of the five or six area colleges that field athletic programs—to speak with FTOs about how best to reach young people. The format works; my dad constantly says that he runs the Fourth Precinct like a football hierarchy: he is the head coach, his lieutenants are coordinators, and his sergeants are position coaches. For him, it's about getting everybody up to speed so they in turn can get their own reports up to speed. There are no expectations for elite pass/fail standards, just a baseline for creating as many good, competent cops as possible.

Sir Robert Peel is the father of modern law enforcement, setting up the first true police force in 1829 London. His goal was for communities to police themselves, but in America, everything was already too screwed up for that to truly happen. Early policing in this country occurred in the form of slave patrols, organized to hunt runaways and brutally accost free Black people. After the Civil War, those patrols were replaced by racist militias whose purpose was to enforce codes at local and state levels designed to keep Black people powerless by restricting things like voting rights, where they could live, and what kind of jobs they could hold. The Fourteenth Amendment, guaranteeing equal protection for all citizens, shepherded in Jim Crow laws, and in the early 1900s, local police departments were established across the country to enforce them.

With all that in mind, it's impossible to talk about police reform without addressing the issue of race. Today, when a cop sees a group of Black males on a street corner, it's second nature to ask for IDs. It's not so different than asking for a letter from their master. The presumption of today's cops, a direct holdover from the slave-patrol mentality, is that those guys are up to no good. In the days of slavery, Black people were not allowed to gather in groups bigger than three for that very reason. We don't realize how much of the modern police mindset dates back to that time. Hell, we drive around in *patrol* cars. It might be time to change our terminology as well as our methodology.

Minneapolis is 18.4 percent Black. The Minneapolis Police Department is 9 percent Black. Back in 1989, when my dad was in charge of recruitment for the department, he put together a nearly all-Black class, including twenty-one people of color. The chief pushed back on that as being a stigma for those recruits, to which Dad responded by saying, well, we've had tons of all-white classes, so what's the difference? You couldn't put a class like that together today, simply because the recruitment numbers aren't there. My own class had two African Americans, including me, and things have only grown worse. A lot of my homeboys left the force after the George Floyd incident, accepting their share of $25.9 million in PTSD settlements, with an average payout of $167,000 per officer. The departure of African American officers from the MPD has been balanced somewhat by the integration of Somalis onto the force—a vital step, given that Minnesota is home to the largest Somali population in the United States. Minority representation, including women, still isn't great, but it's getting better.

Why is this important? In the big picture, as a Black officer working in my community, even when I encountered somebody who didn't much like cops, I usually had at least some benefit of the doubt. He was Black, and so was I. That detail alone was enough to get his attention. People want to see people who look like them, who they feel care for them, who understand what they're going through during a time of need. That's why it's important for us to be reflective. Sometimes, all you need is a small opening.

The entire civic approach toward police has shifted since George Floyd. People still want law enforcement, except they're now reluctant to call 911 and trigger what seems to them like the real risk of a critical incident once an officer shows up. People on the Northside call my dad directly instead of dialing the emergency line, hoping that might make a difference. I'm not just talking about random citizens, either. Now that they no longer have access to SROs, the principals at both our area high schools have dialed Inspector Adams instead of 911 during traumatic moments. With 911, anyone might respond, which, as unlikely as it might be, means you're putting your students in jeopardy in case you get an officer unprepared to deal with kids, and who might inadvertently sabotage the situation. If they call Dad personally, he'll at least send somebody he knows is appropriate for the assignment. If a bad outcome occurs anyway, at least those principals don't have the weight of 911 on their shoulders.

In 2013, the Bureau of Justice Statistics reported that across the country, 71 training hours per officer are devoted to weaponry, and another 60 to self-defense. Those numbers—more than 130 hours combined—square with my own experience. Less than a third of that amount is spent on things like conflict management and diversity training. Given that nearly three in four officers never once discharge their weapons in the course of duty, that ratio seems imbalanced. I want a force that prioritizes effective communication with people over gunning those same people down.

Where I come from, the main impediment to effective communication comes from white cops in Black neighborhoods, few of whom show up at crime scenes with a firm understanding of how to approach the people there. Fear plays a big part; the police are outnumbered and worried that something they say or do might be taken the wrong way. This is not all white cops, of course. Dad's old partner, Lt. Richard Zimmerman, became one of the city's best homicide detectives because as a white man he had no trouble wading into a Black crowd and talking to people respectfully, on their level. He wasn't scared, and he managed to pick up amazing amounts of critical information in the process. On the flip side, I've seen many white officers busy themselves maintaining a crime scene in order to avoid speaking to anybody at all. I've learned the hard way that even if the first person you approach—or the second, or the fifth, or the tenth—ignores you or even greets you with hostility, there's always somebody with information who's willing to talk. You just have to be open to finding it.

It all ties in to the bias implicit in the system. Dad told me about sitting in a training meeting back when he was a rookie, and listening to the cadre officers in charge explain how North Minneapolis is the most dangerous part of the city. He nodded along until one of them said that you'll die quicker in North Minneapolis than in any other part of the city, and that "there ain't nothing worse than getting in a fight with a Black bitch." Uh oh. Dad started wondering what the fuck the message actually was. This guy had no idea Dad was from North Minneapolis or that his mother was one of those Black women he'd so crudely described. That's when Dad realized he'd been playing right into their bullshit all along. They were racist—maybe they didn't understand that, but they most certainly were—and fearful of the Black community. It colored everything they did on the job. That was the start of Dad's refusal to automatically buy into established protocol, a refusal that carries on to this day. He can work within the system—that he's risen almost as high up the ranks as he possibly can is testament to that—but he doesn't for a minute offer blind trust. I support him fully in that.

Want another example? Dad has a million of them, from every level of the Minneapolis Police Department. When he was in charge of the MPD's training program, he helped build scenarios for recruits. One involved a drug deal where Dad played a college professor, and a white guy was harassing him to buy dope. When the trainees showed up and found the drugs on the ground, not knowing who was who, 90 percent of the time they'd arrest Dad.

Where does this fear come from? In reality, not many Black folks shoot at cops. Every intentional police shooting I can think of came at the hands of white radicals. Still, when white officers visit Black neighborhoods, they tend to recoil. That's based more on perception than reality, but it's not surprising. It's what they've been taught. That's why we see so many officer-involved shootings of unarmed Black civilians. Trigger fingers get twitchy when you're concerned for your own safety. People say all the time that white cops are out to kill Black people, but I don't think that's the case. It's straight fear.

As a Black officer, I understood that when African Americans yell at each other, it rarely turns into a fight. That's how Black people operate: they vent. It's a cultural thing. When a Black person goes silent, though? *That's* when you should worry. On the Northside, that's essential knowledge, but it still evades many white cops, who intervene in Black people's business in unproductive ways. I've heard similar things about African American officers patrolling Somali neighborhoods in Minneapolis. Because it's a different culture, one where people aren't even speaking English, it's only natural for an outsider to wonder which confrontations might lead to violence. That happened to my dad: he was riding with a Somali officer who was on the force thanks in part to a dedicated effort by the MPD to recruit members of the East African community. When Dad questioned whether they should get involved in a street-side dispute, his partner began to laugh. "They're just arguing over politics," he said with a smile. Basic understanding can help avoid so much unnecessary confrontation. (Even within the Somali population of Minneapolis, we've seen that while members of the community tend to open up to their countrymen on the police force, when it comes to issues of domestic abuse, Somali women generally trust those male officers *less* than their US-born counterparts, fearing the East African boys club might trump the law. It took some trial and error to learn that Black female officers get a much better response from women of that community.)

I even heard about a police chief in a southern state who made a policy of salt-and-pepper squad cars—a white cop riding with a Black cop—in an ongoing cultural exchange effort. There's some validity to that, and little downside.

One way to gauge how a police department is doing in this regard is to study the citizen complaints lodged against it. The Minneapolis Police Department makes this information publicly available. Between 2013 and 2022, the MPD received nearly five thousand complaints, broken down nearly equally between Black citizens and white citizens. Black people, however, reported excessive use of force at nearly twice the rate of whites, and they were nearly three times likelier to report harassment and discrimination. Whites lodged more complaints than Blacks about things like inappropriate language and failure to provide protection. Things might be changing, though;

excessive-force complaints on the Northside have dropped as of late. Dad says he hasn't seen one all year. Body cameras have had a huge effect, not necessarily in preventing officers from doing stupid things, but in allowing the department to discover it when they do, and then reprimand, suspend, and fire them as necessary. Come on, you *know* you're on camera and you're doing that stuff anyway? What we've been through the last three years has also had an effect. No officer wants to be the next story.

One path toward cultural understanding is having police work the areas they're from. Connection with residents is among the most powerful crime-deterrent tools available. If I know people on the scene, I'm less afraid to interact with them on a meaningful level, not to mention I'm less inclined to shoot them. There is a downside, of course, to having criminals know where you live, but that shouldn't be an issue for cops who treat people respectfully. It's built-in restraint. Don't go cracking heads or talking crazy. I myself embrace that mantra because everybody knows where to find me. I'm at the football field every day at three o'clock. I don't hide.

Sean McGinty, inspector of the Third Precinct, said that things could have been a whole lot worse the night his head-quarters burned down if it wasn't for the relationship that my dad and Chief Medaria Arradondo (a fifth-generation Minnesotan who'd gone to Roosevelt High School on the Southside) had with the Black community. When Dad heard about marchers coming toward the Fourth Precinct—this is after they'd already burned down the Third—he called up Reverend Jerry McAfee for help. The precinct was filled with cops, but Dad wanted to avoid unnecessary confrontation while the city was still on fire. The reverend was well connected through his New Salem Missionary Baptist Church, and he mobilized a Black motorcycle club for support. Those guys rolled up, and sure enough they kept the protestors off the building without inflaming tensions. They'd been patrolling quite a bit during the riots, preventing all sorts of arson. I think it's important to emphasize here that the vast majority of arsonists during the riots—the ones who burned the Third, who wanted to burn the Fourth, and who did so much damage across Minneapolis—were largely white. Everybody can picture the brothers and sisters running from stores with all their loot, but it wasn't them breaking out windows and setting fires. That all originated from a bunch of white instigators, many of whom didn't even live in Minneapolis.

Not long thereafter, Chief Arradondo went to the heart of the discord, George Floyd Square, and on national TV removed his hat and publicly apologized to the Floyd family. That took some guts, and some heart. At the funeral, he bent to one knee and put his head down as the procession started. The intention was to promote trust and respect between police and the community. It's worth noting that all three of those guys—Dad, Arradondo, and McGinty—are Minneapolis natives. It's also worth noting that the white officer who took a knee alongside Dad, Commander Dave O'Connor, received a lot of grief for that action from white officers on the force, and, though he'd been an MPD lifer, left the department soon thereafter.

I'll give you one more example. When my sister, Brittney, was stationed in the Third Precinct, post–George Floyd, she encountered a steady stream of abuse—not from African American locals, but from white women from wealthy Southwest Minneapolis wearing Black Lives Matter T-shirts, who consistently gave her attitude for no reason beyond the uniform she wore. In her eyes, those people were hijacking a Black issue from a neighborhood beyond their own. It reached the point that Dad got Brittney out of there, bringing her to the Fourth Precinct, the Northside, where despite markedly higher levels of street violence she felt safer among the population. It's easy to see why: she's built relationships in that community not only as a police officer, but as a dean at North High before that and as a kid growing up on the streets before that. Brittney has loved those people for decades, and they love her right back. She told me about one raucous murder scene where a female bystander actually hit her with her purse. My sister didn't even have to respond. "You don't do that to Miss Brittney," somebody in the crowd shouted, pulling the woman away and allowing Brittney to do her job. Just like that, a situation that could easily have escalated was diffused.

Another time, one of my ex-players was resisting officers' attempts to get him into the back seat of a squad car when Brittney arrived. "Get your ass back there," she barked. He quickly complied. The other cops couldn't believe it. When they asked how she did it, the answer was simple: "It's a North High thing." Whatever trouble that guy was in, he respected my sister. When Brittney worked as a detention officer at the Hennepin County Jail, an inmate once cursed her out over enforcing some rules infraction. He was immediately shut down by another

inmate—my former wide receiver, Jamin. "You don't talk to Brittney like that," he said. "She's family." The guy not only backed
down, but apologized. Community can be a powerful tool.

The Minneapolis Police Department is full of entrenched white
guys who do things that are labeled racist by outsiders, but as
I've said, I'm not sure that's what's going on. The department
has its share of assholes, but is there an abundance of actual racists? The way I see it, I would say no. More like a lot of Archie
Bunkers. Archie Bunker, from *All in the Family*, was regressive
and wrong about so many things, but he was real with his feelings and up front about it all. Back in the day, African Americans loved that show for that very reason. Archie was genuine
to himself, and for that my parents' generation respected him.
That's the kind of police bigotry I encountered during my time
on the force—not outright hatred of other races or cultures so
much as an enduring refusal to understand them. It's the same
at police departments across the country. Law enforcement was
built on top of that ignorance, and it's what officers learn when
they come on board.

If there's a coherent argument to be made against officers
working in their own communities, at least for too much time, it
was presented by Janeé Harteau, MPD's chief in the 2010s. She
had a policy that officers must switch precincts after six years,
which I think was smart for one reason: when you're in the same
precinct for ten or fifteen years, it's easy to become cynical. On

staffs made up of long-timers, people are constantly complaining, and everybody always seems to be pissed off. The Chief did that, the inspector did this . . . who would even want to work in this fucking place? I've heard it myself, over and over. It's one big bitch session, a culture that's constantly upset, and it's nearly impossible to avoid joining in. New officers get caught in the cycle and end up adopting that same attitude without even understanding that it's happening. And if officers are that negative with each other inside the precinct, what kind of attitude do you think they bring out to the community? I realize this contradicts my previous theory about the benefit of officers working within their own communities, but in reality, only a small percentage of police actually work in the areas where they grew up. Even for them, deep knowledge about one part of town can benefit a transfer to someplace else. Growing up in the Fourth gave me a pretty good understanding about how the rest of the precincts worked, too; I was also an effective patrolman in the Second, Third, and Fifth.

A few years back, Dad told me about a meeting he'd attended in which a lieutenant from the Third Precinct raised that very issue, talking about how his older officers, particularly the ones on middle shift, were loaded with terrible attitudes. He requested that group be broken up—either moved inside or dispersed to other precincts around the city. No action was taken. One of those officers was Derek Chauvin.

I never became that jaded, maybe because I spent so much of my police career as the SRO at North. Even from a distance, however, I could see the positive effect of Harteau's precinct-shifting policy. That kind of move prolongs careers. Perpetual complaints disappear. I've actually heard officers confess that, shit, they needed something like that.

It all ties in with the emotional health of the department. Officers are under enough stress as it is, and after the last few fraught years in Minneapolis, there's no denying they're unwell. Men and women have departed the force in droves under the weight of PTSD, brought on or amplified by the riots. And it's not like those who stayed are immune.

Think about it this way: a cop shows up at a homicide scene, and the mother of the victim breaks down in his arms, inconsolable. It is emotionally trying, but before the officer can unpack whatever impact that violence and its aftermath may have had on him, he must head to his next call and then to the call after that, his day filled with victimized citizens and the occasional horrific crime scene. Along the way he may be called a racist, an asshole, or worse. As soon as he's off the street, he has to go write up his reports. Then he comes back the next day and does it all over again.

One of my colleagues was once called to attend to a young girl who'd been shot in the head while bouncing on a trampoline in her yard. She raced the girl to the hospital herself, then stood by helplessly as the child passed away. No therapist ever talked to her about it. That same cop also saved a kid's life by administering a tourniquet after he'd been shot in the leg. Nobody talked to her about that, either. Speaking personally, I once responded to a house fire call to find paramedics giving CPR to a five-year-old boy they'd dragged out. My own son, Adrian, was about that age then, and in that moment it was as if I was looking directly at him. All I could see was his face. Then it was on to the next.

It's a lot of input, and these men and women have little idea about how to balance it all. Most can't even go home and talk to their spouses about what they've seen because they need that space to hold the normal parts of their lives. On the occasions I took it home—not directly sharing, but showing my frustration—my wife would shut me down with a quick "I'm not somebody off the street, don't talk to me like that." I was in cop mode and had to be put in my place. For a lot of police, stress at work leads to stress at home, which cycles back around to work. It can be vicious. If each precinct in Minneapolis had a full-time therapist on staff, I'm convinced we wouldn't be down three hundred officers. Not only could people acquire tools to make sense of whatever happens, but institutional recognition of mental health can help promote the idea that it's more than a personal struggle—that everybody goes through it to one degree or another.

It adds up to cops repeatedly doing things that make us all look bad. Minneapolis police are intimately aware of the shame visited upon Derek Chauvin and his fellow officers, up to and including imprisonment. Nobody in the department wants a similar fate, yet they continue to get into trouble. To my mind, the main reason for this is that they haven't unpacked their abundant emotional baggage.

There's actually a way for departments to assess those kinds of things before they become problematic. The MPD used to have one. It was called the Early Intervention System, a data-driven management tool designed to help identify problem officers when it came to things like mental health, as well as race-based or violent tendencies. Let's say a guy calls in sick repeatedly, and complaints are registered about him, and he's getting into it with his shiftmates, and we get reports about his recklessness in the field. Without the EIS system, these signifiers of brewing trouble might fall through the cracks. If all of that was documented, though, and filtered appropriately, his sergeant would be alerted to a potential problem, and the department could provide necessary support before the officer did something truly regrettable.

The EIS system was monitored by a lieutenant and a civilian who reported to my dad. The operation seemed to be working, but someone in the hierarchy didn't like it and the plan was abandoned before it could even get up to speed. The computerized database has been sitting dormant ever since. They're just now getting around to figuring out how to update it with current software.

After George Floyd, I myself started to second-guess my line of work, wondering why I was a policeman at all. That was a tough place to be after nearly two decades on the job. I'd been a clear target during those riots, and I still couldn't definitively answer why I was out there to begin with. Was our police presence even the right thing? More than a year after the riots, the Fourth Precinct, where I reported for work after my SRO job was eliminated, was still surrounded by temporary fencing, boards covering up the windows to protect against the people we were allegedly there to serve. It all fused into a multipronged crisis for me—of confidence, of career, of mortality.

Thanks to the opportunity to become head of player security for the Twins, my crisis didn't last long. Whatever improvements the MPD might make will have to happen without me.

Much of the police's recruitment problem starts with its own public image. People base their perceptions less on personal interactions than on video clips and online commentary, and to that end, social media tends to be unkind to people in my line of work. Sometimes it's necessary, as when it was used to spread the horrifying images of Derek Chauvin atop George Floyd, spurring justified outcry about police practices. Far more frequently it distorts reality for the sake of outrage. I don't need to look further than my coaching staff at North High to see it.

Tim Lawrence, my offensive line coach, is a lieutenant with the Metro Transit Police Department, for whom he has worked since 2012. Tim found himself in some hot water in 2018, when video of his confrontation with a bus passenger went viral. Tim is white, and the lady with whom he got into it was Black. The three-minute clip shows the woman with her arm wrapped around a bus shelter post, doing all she can to withstand what looks like police aggression while Tim pins her opposite arm. When she tries to pull away, he engages a straight arm-bar takedown, drops her to the ground, and cuffs her.

Backlash was intense. People called for boycotts of Metro Transit buses, and Tim's name was dragged all over town, with repeated calls for his firing. Except that people only knew—maybe only wanted to know—part of the story.

The incident started downtown, at Eighth and Hennepin, when the woman confronted the bus driver, apparently over a refusal to pull over between stops so she could disembark, then proceeded to harass the driver to the point that the police were called. That's when Tim showed up. When he asked the driver what she wanted, he was told simply to get the woman off the bus. Okay, easy enough. That's basic policing: if you get called to a house for a domestic disturbance, you don't leave both people in there together. When Tim asked the woman to depart, she instead chose to retreat deeper into the interior of the bus.

Tim followed, told her that the next bus would arrive within ten minutes, and requested that she exit quietly and wait for it. Had the woman listened, the incident would have ended there. Instead, she responded with a stream of curses, this time directed at Tim. Tim is not one to easily lose his composure, and he continued to peacefully urge her outside. More cursing. The third time he asked, the woman finally complied, but despite being steps from the rear door, she attempted to exit through the front, in order to gain proximity to the driver. Tim shut that down, at which point the woman spit toward the driver—that's fourth-degree assault—and said, "You fucking white devil, I'm going to find you and kill you." Now she'd gone from disorderly conduct to issuing terroristic threats. The driver quickly indicated she wanted to press charges. That's why Tim was trying to get the lady's ID near the bus stop, which is when the YouTube video begins. Even after she took out her ID, she taunted him with it, yanking it back every time he tried to have a look. Her resistance went against every rule of thumb I recommend to my community for dealing with police. Ultimately, she could have gone peacefully on her way if she'd listened to Tim in the first place. Instead, she ended up in handcuffs, in the back of a squad car.

Tim is a good guy and far from abusive. We've talked policing many times, and he's told me repeatedly about how he's focused his entire career on not being *that* guy, and treating people with dignity and respect. It's not just talk—he'd been named Metro Transit's Officer of the Year the year before the incident. The clip that was shared so many times showed only the final stages of the confrontation, and none of the lead-up, nor the fact that Tim was able to subdue the woman safely using minimum force. That the officer who arrived for backup unholstered her Taser drew significant criticism as well, never mind that she never even powered it up let alone used it.

To cops watching that clip, the interaction did not look like abuse—just an officer trying to do his job with somebody intent on impeding his progress. Honestly, if I were a bus driver, I hope police would respond the same way if somebody spat at me. When the clip went viral, Tim called me immediately. "I know I didn't do anything wrong," he said, "but I don't want this to blow back at North, and I don't want the guys on the team to feel any differently about me." He had real concerns about being a white cop accused of racial violence while coaching a mostly Black team. He asked me what he should do. "Get your ass up here to practice," I told him.

A bunch of players had already seen the clip before Tim arrived, and they greeted him warmly. "Hey coach, we saw it," I heard them say. "Man, you did everything right." When practice broke down into position groups, he discussed it with the offensive linemen, even queueing up the video for them so they could make up their own minds. Not one player took issue with what had happened. Honestly, the incident was over almost before it started, not only among our coaches and players, but with the entire North High community. We all knew that Tim was nothing like the monster social media was making him out to be. In a world where people communicate in person and take the time to explain things that matter, his reputation held up just fine.

North High players know they can trust the people around them. Even in the wake of George Floyd—*especially* in the wake of George Floyd—they see police officers up close every day on our practice field, and recognize firsthand that we are not all the same. Even within our coaching group, I'm different than my dad, who is different than Tim, who is different than Rick Plunkett. Kids are able to view us distinctly while understanding that, amid our differences, our similarities make up the most important pieces of the equation. We all care deeply about our players, and none of us will ever put them in a situation counter to their own best interests.

That insight helps those kids interact with random police outside of school, because no matter what they've seen on TV, they understand that cops are people, too. It actually works on both sides of the equation, as officers who encounter those boys on the street tend to give them the benefit of the doubt upon learning they play football for me at North High.

As coaches and policemen, we instruct our players about how to handle interactions with law enforcement. Even if the officer is aggressive or mean, respect is paramount. If you've been pulled over, turn off the car, keep your hands on the steering wheel, and quietly listen to whatever they tell you. Make no sudden movements. Kids are quick to suggest that if the cop is disrespectful, they'll respond in kind. Okay, if you want things to end badly, that's just what to do. Otherwise, keep your mouth shut. Legitimate grievances about the cop can be taken to the precinct or to court, where the chances of actually being heard— let alone not being arrested, beaten, or shot—swing markedly in your favor.

It's not just kids. My dad was once pulled over in his BMW while off duty. He'd just renewed his license and had only a temporary slip of paper to show the officer. Before the guy went to run it, Dad asked why he'd been pulled over in the first place. "Your driver's license is expired," the cop explained. "That's why you have this temporary one." Dad asked how he came by that information.

"I ran your plates," the officer said.

"What was your probable cause for running my plate?" Dad asked.

That gave the officer pause. "Are you a cop?" he asked.

"Yes I am, out of the Chief's office," said Dad, who worked for the mayor at the time. "I'll ask again, what was your PC for running my plate?" As the guy stammered his way through a nonanswer, Dad cut him off.

"Let me tell you something," he said. "I taught traffic stops at the state academy. I probably taught *your* ass. Now, for the third time: What was your probable cause for running my plate?" At that point the cop returned his license and walked away. Dad never even filed a complaint, thinking that the interaction taught that cop the necessary lesson.

Not everybody has the same insider knowledge as my father, but even with a genuine grievance, Officer Adams hewed to the rules of the game. When that policeman approached his car, the engine had been turned off and Dad's hands were on the wheel, in plain view. Dad had some grilling to do, but he spoke respectfully throughout the interaction. Sure, if Dad had been a plumber or a dentist or something, he would not have been able to direct the situation so thoroughly, but his respect for authority would have been a constant, no matter his line of work.

When Chief Janeé Harteau took over the Minneapolis Police Department in 2012, she unveiled something called MPD 2.0, a strategic plan to address abundant issues within the department: oversight, discipline, transparency, and accountability. She launched programs to train officers in procedural justice (treating citizens respectfully and explaining why they do what they do during moments of tension) and implicit bias (recognizing one's own biases in police work, and working through the biases of others). She emphasized diversity, with the goal of making the MPD more resemble the communities it serves. She implemented performance reviews and renewed focus on outreach, growing the Police Activities League and hiring a community engagement coordinator. She ran "safety summits" on the Northside and Southside to get community members involved in the department's efforts toward reducing crime in their neighborhoods.

Unfortunately, the main thing I remember about 2.0 was how little the people in the department thought of it. A lot of officers didn't take it seriously. Most of it was pretty much how we did police work anyway, so, internally, the plan was seen merely as an effort to change public perception. I'm sure there was some progress made, but the Chief's plan was never fully accepted. Any genuinely new initiatives didn't work because officers were stuck in their ways; the standard response within the ranks when somebody proposes a new policy is, "Cops don't like change." That gives them an excuse to more or less ignore it. A plan will never amount to much if people within the department won't abide by it, no matter how ambitious or forward-thinking it may be. That was MPD 2.0's downfall. Even though the details made sense, too many people in key positions simply didn't give a fuck about changing things up.

Chief Harteau's departure in 2017 meant the effective end of 2.0. Every chief brings his or her own plan, and 2.0 was replaced by Chief Arradondo's focus on procedural justice, which received about the same response among the ranks as 2.0. Numerous

aspects of both initiatives continued until George Floyd. That
was the end of many of those programs; when the department's
funding got slashed, vital initiatives simply went away.

This might be why, ten years after 2.0 was instituted, we've
seen multiple reports from both state and federal agencies
ripping the department to shreds. The most newsworthy one,
which was released by the Justice Department in June 2023,
spent eighty-nine pages outlining epidemic levels of discrimination and excessive force. Deficiencies were identified in areas
of accountability, training, supervision, and officer wellness
programs. In it, Attorney General Merrick Garland called the
MPD's practices "deeply disturbing," saying that not only do
they erode community trust in law enforcement, but they "made
what happened to George Floyd possible."

It doesn't take long for the report to reach the heart of the
problem. It's right there on page one: "For years, MPD used dangerous techniques and weapons against people who committed
at most a petty offense and sometimes no offense at all. MPD
used force to punish people who made officers angry or criticized
the police. MPD patrolled neighborhoods differently based on
their racial composition and discriminated based on race when
searching, handcuffing, or using force against people during
stops. The City sent MPD officers to behavioral health-related
911 calls, even when a law enforcement response was not appropriate or necessary, sometimes with tragic results. These actions
put MPD officers and the Minneapolis community at risk."

Unreasonable force. Unnecessary discharge of firearms,
sometimes with people in the line of fire. Beating the shit out of

people who presented no threat. Refusing medical aid to people in custody. Failing to intervene when colleagues were doing any or all of that, with officers showing a willful tolerance for inexplicable conduct within their ranks. And we haven't even reached the part about discrimination.

Yeah, just like you could have guessed, Black and brown people bear the brunt of all that abuse. The Justice Department noted that the MPD disproportionately pulls over Black people and Native Americans, after which it disproportionately uses force against them, its patrol styles tending to be dictated by the racial composition of the neighborhood. Maddeningly, rather than change their behavior after George Floyd, officers just stopped documenting race during traffic stops, lest the resulting data somehow come back to bite them. (Just in case anyone thinks this kind of thing is limited to the Minneapolis, the Justice Department investigation in Minneapolis was only the first of eight, with police departments large and small, from Phoenix to Oklahoma City, under similar scrutiny.)

That report was just the latest in a string of official studies offering multiple variations on the same theme. A year earlier, Minnesota's top civil rights enforcement agency, the Department of Human Rights, released its own findings from a two-year study launched in the immediate aftermath of George Floyd's murder. Not surprisingly, it also found the MPD guilty of all kinds of malpractice.

Much of that report overlaps with the Justice Department's findings, while adding some wrinkles of its own. MPD recruits were taught to view citizens as the enemy, it said, pinning

unnecessary force to more than a quarter of the episodes studied between 2010 and 2020. The report said that officers even
went so far as to hunt protestors—they actually used the word
"hunt"—roaming the city in an unmarked van and firing indiscriminate nonlethal rounds into activist crowds. It said police
undermine public safety rather than uphold it. My dad, who is
much more involved in police procedure than I ever was, takes
issue with many of the state's findings. He feels the person in
charge of compiling the report was biased against the force.
When I read it, however, it rings largely true.

For me, the most disturbing part of the report covered the
MPD's approach to race. Nothing shocked people more than
the headline-grabbing detail that the department more or less
ignored active white nationalists, yet surveilled law-abiding
members of the Black community, in part by using fake social
media accounts and posing as Black citizens to engage with and
criticize elected officials and organizations like the NAACP and
the Urban League. Part of it is as simple as trying to associate
the Black Lives Matter movement with every activist in the city,
lumping multiple organizations into one group, which is either
lazy policing or a way to turn a bunch of law-abiding people
into criminals. There was no public safety objective—just troll-
ing minorities on city time.

The report called out racist language used by officers while
on duty, from the N-word to calling people "monkeys." There
were all sorts of offensive terms for women, used not only
behind closed doors but directly to citizens' faces. The report
detailed excessive attention paid to Black Minneapolitans, who,

while making up 19 percent of the city's population, were sub-
jected to more than half the traffic stops and citations issued
by the MPD, to the point that African Americans have come
to refer to the system as a Black Tax. Because the department
claimed that some of the disparity can be attributed to factors
other than race, the report studied citations issued under similar
circumstances, and found that Black drivers were still 1.5 times
more likely to be cited than whites. Even that number is flawed
because how many similar circumstances are there for cops who
cruise Black neighborhoods passing out tickets for broken taillights? They don't exist.

It gets worse. Black citizens were the subjects of 63 percent
of use-of-force incidents, including suffering neck restraints at
nearly twice the rate of white citizens under similar circumstances, and being maced 25 percent more frequently. When
obstruction was the primary offense, Blacks were maced almost
twice as often as whites.

The outrageous details go on and on. Black drivers were 12
percent more likely to be pulled over during daylight hours than
at night, when it's easier for officers to determine race from a
distance. Police supervisors admitted to a pattern of pulling over
people for no reason at all, simply so the officer could sweep their
vehicle for guns or drugs, which helps explain why Black drivers
were the subject of 78 percent of MPD's vehicle searches. The
report also notes that in other jurisdictions, drugs and weapons are found more frequently in the vehicles of white people
than those driven by people of color. Minneapolis didn't keep
accurate enough records for a similar assessment, though one

resident of color reported being pulled over seven times during a five-year span for minor violations, with officers saying they smelled marijuana on four of those occasions. At each of those junctures he was handcuffed—sometimes with guns drawn—while his vehicle was searched. Drugs were never found. Needless to say, nobody tried to pull that shit in front of me, which is far from saying it didn't happen elsewhere.

The report called out officers for citing citizens with obstruction or disorderly conduct for behavior that, from a legal standpoint, was neither of those things, but which one MPD leader described as falling under the category of "pissing off the police," in whatever noncriminal form that might take. How do we know that many of those charges are trumped up? More Black citizens had their cases dropped or dismissed, or were found not guilty, than white citizens being tried for the same offenses.

Most impactful, 93 percent of officer-involved deaths between January 2020 and February 2022 were people of color. I guess you're bound to get some of that when you have mostly white cops working Black neighborhoods, but that number is utterly shocking.

Then there's this, directly from the report:

"One patrol officer claimed that they did not engage in racial profiling, yet later in the interview provided an example of how they might solve a crime based on racial stereotypes," the report stated. "This officer did not appear to understand that searching for someone based solely on racial stereotypes was, in fact, racial profiling."

If cops don't even know what racial profiling is, much less that they're doing it, that's a direct result of training deficiencies. As a former police officer, I couldn't help but note the finding that officers are twice as likely to be injured themselves when using inappropriate force.

The Justice Department report offered twenty-eight suggestions for improving the MPD, including enhancements to training, accountability, and use of force policies. The Minnesota Department of Human Rights did them one better, securing a court order requiring the MPD to enact several notable policies:

- Ban chokeholds and neck restraints like the one that killed George Floyd.
- Address an officer's duty to intervene should a fellow officer engage in unauthorized use of force, and to report the incident. (Importantly, they designated that this should happen *regardless* of rank and seniority [emphasis theirs]. They found reports against trainers or veteran officers were "rare or nonexistent," to the point that they used a term for it: "unquestioned compliance." Failure to act, they said, makes the observer as culpable as the offender.)
- Limit the use of crowd-control weapons to those directly authorized by the chief.
- Set firm timetables for disciplinary decisions, ensuring that complaints are not endlessly kicked down the road.
- Regularly review body-cam footage to proactively identify discriminatory misconduct.

"Without fundamental organizational culture changes," the report concluded, "reforming MPD's policies, procedures, and trainings will be meaningless."

To be fair, duty to intervene was policy before Chauvin, but it was barely emphasized. Now it's a clear part of the program. Now, officers can't say, "I didn't know." If we'd had that in place sooner, George Floyd might still be alive. Believe me, those officers would act differently if they could do it all over again. That's an easy call, considering they lost their reputations and careers, went to prison, and ended up being villains to the world.

I'll take being a villain to the cops over being a villain to the world every single time.

In late 2021, the mayor put together a twenty-two-member community-safety workgroup consisting of experts, community members, and "public safety practitioners," with the goal of reforming the police department. I was one of them. We met once in person and then via a series of subcommittee Zoom sessions every two or three weeks for about five months. Those meetings were productive. My subcommittee was involved with police procedures and field training, and my area of input concerned the FTO process, and how to better prepare the department to create good, capable officers. Implementing a system for reporting misconduct—the type of EIS program we've been sitting on for years, which would include FTO training missteps—was a key feature of our vision for the department.

In June 2022, our report was released. What did we get right? Much like the Minnesota Department of Human Rights, we identified racist and discriminatory policing practices, including racial profiling, and called for increased oversight, accountability, and transparency. We called for an end to aggressive and abusive policing practices. We even looked beyond the police, at potential programs that address income and education disparities within the community, stating outright that "the lingering effects of redlining, marginalization, and exclusion of people of color have compounded the issues of policing and safety within our city."

So far, so good.

As it happened, some of the best suggestions came from our citizens' forum, in which we fielded recommendations from the general public. Those included holding MPD officers more accountable, focusing on youth engagement, and putting a stronger emphasis on officer recruitment. One comment that stuck with me was, "MPD needs to be trusted by the community." This speaks to the importance of things like the Police Activities League (PAL), where I coached for so many years, which is finally making a comeback after being nearly completely defunded.

My panel determined that recruitment could be improved by providing candidates with access to mentors and support services, and by better utilizing courses designed by adult-learning experts. We suggested stringent criteria for FTO qualification and better guidelines for the leadership overseeing the program.

We also suggested eliminating all "warrior-type training" from MPD courses.

To the department's credit, it has begun to implement a number of the panel's ideas. Officers are now instructed to use the minimum level of force necessary. (When I was in the academy, we were taught to treat threats as more severe than they actually were.) Chokeholds and neck restraints have been banned. (That was a work in progress when I was on the force.) They also did away with the kind of no-knock warrants that allow for the type of unannounced breaking down of doors that ended Amir Locke's life. Officers have been barred from pulling over vehicles for things like expired tabs and broken license plate lights. It's almost as if they wrote that part for me.

One development that gives me particular hope is the adoption of the Active Bystandership for Law Enforcement (ABLE) program, which was developed by the Georgetown University Law Center in part to fix a generations-long mindset that discourages officers from speaking out against the misdeeds of their colleagues. (That's the "bystandership" part of the title.) Instead of framing it as ratting, trainees are taught to view the process as a preventative measure to help fellow cops who might be overtired, overworked, or otherwise not thinking as clearly as they might under better circumstances. It's positioned as a tool to build bonds, not break them, which seems sensible to me. Hundreds of police departments nationwide have signed on to ABLE; the MPD incorporated it into its academy training program at the end of 2021.

Ultimately, despite its abundant flaws, I think the department was on relatively solid footing before everything went to hell. We kept the city safe while doing more good than harm. To me, Derek Chauvin is more outlier than symptom, even though that's hardly the popular perception. I was heartened during his trial when somebody wondered earnestly where the thin blue line had gone, because so many police officers were open books in court. They told the truth and did not make excuses. That's an unquestionably good development. It's no longer like it was back in the day, when cops would do whatever it took to cover each other's asses. The stakes are just too high, and there are too many ways to be exposed.

In the end, for me, it comes down to one thing: it's impossible to make a perfect police department, but there are a million ways to make a good one. Here's hoping MPD is on its way.

Chapter 10

———

The Master Is You

After the 2022 high school football season, I was chosen for the first time to be an assistant coach for the Minnesota High School All-Star Game, featuring the best players from every division in the state. It was a personal honor, to be sure, and even more so it was a nod to the sustained excellence of the North High program. We conducted a week of daily practices, and I got really excited as game day approached.

My high lasted until midway through the second quarter.

The game was held at U.S. Bank Stadium in Minneapolis, and my team, North (not North High School, but the north part of the state, which was playing South), was getting badly beaten, outhustled, outmanned, and flat-out pushed around by a more physical opponent. When the whistle sounded to end the first half, we trailed 16–0, which probably wouldn't have worried me had it been my own team. This roster, though, was different.

In the halftime locker room, players seemed mostly interested in pointing fingers. There's an informal agreement that All-Star teams won't stunt or blitz while on defense, and South was doing both those things, to great effect. Okay, so what? It's not like our players were unfamiliar with the concepts—they all faced those kinds of schemes during the regular season. Now that they were getting their asses kicked, all they wanted to talk about was the other team's dirty play. They didn't say a thing about how our receivers weren't catching the ball and our running backs weren't hitting their holes. South's defense was good, and we weren't stepping up to meet it. The other team played harder than us. Our deficit was a collective effort.

Under normal circumstances I might have ripped into my players at halftime, but I wasn't the head coach and that wasn't my place. Besides, only one guy was from North High, so who knows how that kind of message would have landed with a bunch of kids who didn't know me. As the head coach was addressing the room, I carefully watched players' reactions, too many of which were utterly indifferent. Finally, I had to say *something*. When the coach paused, I piped up and asked if I could speak. He gave a nod, and I laid it out.

"You guys are making too many excuses," I told the players. "You're focusing on the rules and what things the other team is doing. What you're not doing is being football players. You're getting pushed around out there, and all you want to do is point fingers." My message was one of accountability—how, if the North squad took care of its own business instead of worrying about the other team, things would improve.

I don't think anybody heard me. We lost the game, 29–0.

The mindset in that locker room reminds me of my favorite movie, Berry Gordy's *The Last Dragon*, from 1985. I watched that thing over and over when I was a kid. It's about a Black martial-arts teenager in New York City named Leroy Green, who, to reach the final level of his training, is instructed to search for the ultimate master. "There is one place that you have not looked," his sensei tells him, "and it is there, only there, that you shall find [him]." In the end, Leroy learns that the place he has not looked is inward, and that he himself is the ultimate master. I wish my All-Star team had more of that attitude.

What really bothered me, far more than the score, was the players' sense of entitlement. You haven't succeeded in your assignment, and your response is to blame others? Our roster featured forty-four players from forty-one high schools, and there was no unified system to keep them together. That's the nature of All-Star games. With that kind of structure (or lack thereof), it's easy for bad attitudes to snowball when things go wrong. I bring it up here because those concepts are just as true for the entire Northside as they are for a football team.

My neighborhood consistently faces issues that people in other parts of the city rarely have to consider. Gang violence affects nearly everybody, even though only a tiny percentage of residents are affiliated with gangs. Our families tend to struggle financially, with too many single moms working too many low-paying jobs. We have a surplus of renters and not enough homeowners, too much crime and not enough quality health care. The structure to keep it all contained simply doesn't exist.

I'm not saying anything here that people don't already know. The question is how to approach it.

It's easy to point fingers. Lord knows, folks on the Northside have plenty of places to point. They have been treated like second-class citizens since before the redlining that created the neighborhood in the first place. But what does blaming others get you? The same thing it got my All-Star team: nothing. Energy spent complaining or demonizing others is energy not spent on bettering one's situation. Malcolm X said, "There is no better teacher than adversity." To me, there's a difference between losing and failure. Losing is a lesson; it's only failure if you take nothing from it.

Why did I write this book? In part, to show what Black success can be. I was raised on the Northside and remain wholly invested in the neighborhood's success, earning whatever respect I've been given by prioritizing my people, be it as a cop, a football coach, or simply a man who loves his community. Black excellence is attainable. People need to want it.

It's easy to say that there are many paths to prosperity, but the first step is defining the term. So many kids from North High and beyond have limited vision of their own futures, too easily accepting the idea that much of society is off-limits to them. The notion of becoming doctors or executives or airline pilots doesn't even cross their minds. Even the concept of community college is beyond the scope of many people. It doesn't have to be that way, but our circumstances present so many immediate needs that little space is left to look toward the long term.

I was fortunate. My parents were both educated, and my father was dedicated to providing a positive example of what might be. That became vital once I had my own family. As I went through my issues at the academy, all I could think about was how I was going to take care of my wife and kids. Because my wife, Andreaua, sacrificed her professional ambitions to raise our children, it became my responsibility to bring home a paycheck. I took that seriously.

Unfortunately, too many kids in my neighborhood come from single-parent homes, where their mothers work low-paying jobs that leave them treading water, and any examples provided by their fathers are often the wrong kind. That's one reason I pay so much attention to how I carry myself through day-to-day life. Kids are watching. When my dad barred me from playing football my junior year because my grades were down, I resented him for it. Now, I understand. Integrity is everything.

Success can take many forms. Not every kid can go to college, or even wants to. Rather than settling for a dead-end job, so many young people could find success by setting out on a career path. Being involved in a trade, be it a medical technician or a pipe fitter or even a police officer, a stable job with benefits is within the reach of everybody—if only they could see it. I think about my dad's decision to leave a solid job with Metro Transit, taking a pay cut to join the MPD. He had a big-picture vision of a future that the transit department simply couldn't provide—a vision I see lacking with so many people in our neighborhood. They settle for whatever they're able to get in the moment and rarely aspire to anything more. You don't have to settle for being a convenience-store clerk just because it's right in front of you. I wish more people understood that.

At North High, sports keep kids connected to the outside world, opening their eyes to opportunities. The team experience lets them connect with people across the state and see how people who live differently than them go about their business. It opens up their landscape beyond the Northside in ways they might not have otherwise been able to access.

That said, opportunities at the school aren't limited to sports. North High has numerous options for exploring theater and the arts, for taking leadership programs and studying abroad. When I was a high school student, I took advantage of citywide student government and groups like drug-free athletes. The more involved you are, the more you understand the world around you. It's all about utilizing the resources within your community. "Stay busy to stay out of trouble" is one of my favorite sayings. I wish we could all emphasize that just a little bit more.

The Northside is my foundation, the key that starts the car. It is why I am who I am. I have to be careful, though, because as much as I love the Northside, it doesn't always love me back. When I was North High's school resource officer, my profession was policeman but my role was community caretaker, and I accepted it with all seriousness. That's a huge part of why I was good at the job. Still, after George Floyd, many community members—friends, people on the school board, even some of my wife's family members—turned against me because of the patch on my uniform. I can't help but think if they truly saw me and understood what I was about, they never would have taken those positions.

By voting in favor of terminating their contract with the MPD and removing SROs from schools, the school board lumped every cop on the force in with Derek Chauvin, which made me sick. The vote had nothing to do with me personally, but it was impossible to take it any other way. Critics didn't want us around kids and were willing to overlook our individual reputations and our community's need to get their way. Nobody from the board even reached out to me to have a conversation about it. People were convinced without evidence that the city's students had been traumatized by the Minneapolis Police Department. "We like you," more than one person told me, "but you're part of the problem." At that point I wasn't OA or Spank or Charles, I was just another Minneapolis cop, and we all had to go. To willingly ignore all I'd done for the community was insulting.

Most of the school board members came from places outside my district, but two of them were Northsiders who knew just how negatively that decision would impact our kids. They signed off on the plan anyway. When I pleaded for them to reconsider, they told me there was nothing I could say or do, that it was a done deal. I've never felt more helpless. Not surprisingly, they both lost their reelection campaigns in 2022.

I can't help but think that if more people were invested in their community, that outcome might have been different. That's a persistent problem in poorer neighborhoods. Why look after a place when you have no ownership of it, be it financial or emotional? What's in it for you to pick up litter or help make the parks safe if you feel like you're already at zero before you've begun? Conversely, the more you put into a place, the more you can take out. Even after they ripped my SRO job from me, I still believe that. The Northside is as important to me now as it ever was.

My devotion to community has been unbelievably rewarding, but it has come at a cost. Dedicating so much energy to the high school, the football team, and the police department frequently meant my wife and children were left behind, receiving only the crumbs of me. When I think about sacrifices I've made, they're who I picture. In many ways, my own successes have blinded me to achieving similar things for my family.

I missed most of Adrian's football games his junior and senior years of high school because his team usually played at the same time as North. Practices and other obligations frequently interfered with the events of my daughters, Anyla and Audria. It's not like I was absent from their lives—we lived in the same house and I interacted with them every day—but I didn't do the greatest job giving them top priority. Adrian is now twenty-three and attends Concordia University, St. Paul, where he is a wide receiver on the football team. I've made a point of being in the stands for his home games, and watching his away games on the school's TV feed. Anyla is nineteen, and a freshman at the University of St. Thomas, where she's majoring in nursing and is on the spirit squad. Audria, seventeen, is a junior at Park Center Senior High School near our home in Minneapolis, where she does competitive cheer. Now that most of their activities take place on weekends—Audria's cheer competitions, and football games for both Adrian (playing) and Anyla (cheering)—I prioritize them over most of whatever else I might have going on. The downside is that many of their events overlap. I frequently find myself watching one kid on a screen while I watch another one live.

I am particularly proud that Adrian has dived headlong into athletics, becoming a sports management major with a minor in coaching. I'm part of that template, but it's not only me. My dad coached me when I was young, and he passed along his values to me just as I've tried to pass them to Adrian. At the same time, Anyla is studying nursing, the same as her mom. Like mother like daughter, like father like son.

The 2022 high school football season, which only recently wrapped up as I write this, put a lot of things in perspective for me and my family. It started with questions about how the Polars would handle the tragedy of Deshaun Hill. That part was heartening; players bonded together in new ways and put significant energy into figuring out how best to commemorate their fallen friend. What happened on the field, though, was different. Despite my best efforts, that team was filled with players who cared about themselves more than each other, giving half-efforts in practice while expecting different results in games. It was similar to my experience in the recent All-Star game, and antithetical to how I live my life. That was incredibly difficult for me to swallow, especially because no matter how I tried, I could not change their mindset. When kids pout after a win because they didn't score the game's last touchdown or get a hundred yards rushing, that's not me or my values. That's not the program I built. We were talented, so we won, but it was the most difficult 8–1 season I could imagine.

Toward the end of the schedule, when our games got closer and our victories harder earned, I heard nothing but excuses in that locker room. It wasn't that our opponents were better than us or played with more ferocity, it was that they were dirty or got lucky. I could never seem to get my guys to accept accountability in ways that might improve them as players and people. That was a new experience for me. I'm ashamed to admit it, but I've viewed my family in much the same way my players viewed this season, putting my personal priorities above theirs. Focusing on the individual, not the team.

Was it selfish to devote so much energy to the football program, let alone the high school and the community? Of course it was. I've been able to do a lot of good for the Northside, and I intend for that to continue, but I've realized that focusing my attention to any of those places means it's not on the people

I love best, back at home. This isn't much of a revelation. My eyes were wide open when I made those decisions. I knew the balance. My dad offered a clear example when I was growing up, working hard to provide for me and my siblings. Where our approaches differ is that he turned his extra energy toward family, not the community. There are many things I can still learn from his approach.

Then again, I consider the entire Northside to be my family, so maybe I adopted his approach after all. Still, I now realize that I can't become the kind of positive role model I aspire to be if my wife or kids are left behind. Every football season I put far more energy toward winning the state championship than whatever my kids are doing.

If I could do it again I would delegate more responsibilities, which is a funny thing to say considering how much I already delegate within the football program: I leave practices largely up to my position coaches, and I serve mostly in a supervisory capacity, which allows me to tackle whatever contingencies arise.

At home, Andreaua plays the role of head coach. In running our house, she has sacrificed everything for our kids. I am still learning how to sacrifice myself to accommodate my family.

When I first took over as head coach, North High was on the verge of closing, the team was down to fifteen players, and we hadn't won a game in what seemed like forever. As we began to succeed, we became more attractive. Soon, kids who had been opting for other schools were turning toward North. Before too long, our football program was robust, and North High itself was attracting attention. Every facet of the school improved. Prosperity bred more prosperity.

I would like my players, as they head into the world after graduation, to leverage the same concept. Build yourself up, one success at a time. Do it by going to college, or by getting a job, and constantly examining how to improve your lot. Work toward promotion. Find a better job. Keep trying to better yourself. It never has to end. Always embrace the message from *The Last Dragon*: the master is in the one place you have not looked.

That's more or less the big-picture philosophy I try to impart to my football teams. Players come to me to learn the sport, and I do what I can to help them improve, but I'm not the most important piece. The most vital thing I can leave them with is the idea that "the master is you."

The master is all of us. What a great lesson to learn.

ACKNOWLEDGMENTS

The "Husker Prayer," which you'll find on the very first page of this book, is something our team has been saying before games since 2013, and which the University of Nebraska football team has been saying since 1994 (when, it should be pointed out, they won coach Tom Osborne his first national championship). One of my players, Josh Cunningham, ran across it someplace and asked me whether he might bring it to the Polars. I told him to go with it. These days, whichever kid has the pride to lead us in it is welcome to step up prior to game time. Somebody always does.

Every time I hear it I think about things like honor and perseverance, concepts that are essential to building character well beyond the football field. In case this book hasn't already made it abundantly clear, let me say it again: I'm all about character.

For me, that concept starts with my wife, Andreaua. Her character keeps our whole family going and has since the very beginning. Back when I was a community service officer making $12 an hour, I frequently took the bus to work because, living paycheck to paycheck, we spent our last dollars on milk and diapers for the baby and had nothing left over for gas. Andreaua was okay with that because she knew where I was headed. We'd started out together at community college, me working toward policing and her studying to be a nurse, but she put her career aside to stay home with young Adrian. I wrote earlier about how I sacrificed family time for my personal and professional ambitions; well, Andreaua did the opposite. She delayed school to make sure I got my degree and became a cop, noting that once we had some real income she would be able to focus more on herself. She was nineteen at the time.

Sure enough, when Adrian was two or three, Andreaua went back to nursing school and built a career, even as we had two more children whose care fell mostly on her. Peanut, I want to express my deep gratitude for all the incredible support and love you've shown over the years. Your patience and understanding have been my rock and my power. I am continually impressed by your strength and resilience, and I am blessed to share my life with you. I love you and am so lucky to have you by my side.

Our kids helped keep Andreaua and me strong and together, because even though she was much more hands-on than me, we were both extremely invested in what they were doing. I coached Adrian when he was young, and Andreaua never missed a game.

In fact, she's only ever missed one of his football games and that's because she'd just had surgery and was confined to bed. When I had to be late or miss a game because the Polars were playing at the same time as Adrian, she made sure to fill me in on everything I missed. (Those updates pertained strictly to our son. Andreaua had eyes only for her baby boy.) Our family's backbone started with him and has grown to include his sisters, Anyla and Audria.

My kids can bicker, fuss, and fight, just like any siblings, but the three of them have an extremely tight bond. They stick up for each other. Anyla is a nurturer who inherited her mother's feistiness. I'll never forget when Audria was being bullied at school, and her big sister jumped up to confront her antagonizer. Yeah, Audria wasn't bullied after that. My youngest daughter is so quick-witted, the queen of one-liners who talks the same kind of shit I do. She's kind of a female version of me. Now that Adrian is in college locally and living at home, he's gone right back to his role as peacemaker, always making sure everybody's right. I love my family so much.

I cannot adequately explain how much my father means to me. He is the most influential male figure in my life. I learned how to be a man from his guidance. Even as a kid I tried to enter his sphere of influence wherever possible. When I was thirteen, he let me practice with his flag football team. Once, when they were a man short, I actually got to play in a game—at the Metrodome, no less. I ran up and down that field with so much energy, thrilled to be playing with my dad. I hope this book accurately conveys how much I love him, and how much I owe to him.

My mom, Djuana, is a sweet, kind-hearted person who never says anything bad about anybody. Even though I spent much more time with my father—like I said, I was the only thing he kept when Mom moved across town after their divorce—there's no mistaking her love for me, and mine for her. Mom is especially close with my younger siblings, who went with her while I stayed with Dad. That's as it should be.

My sister Brittney, who's six years younger than me, has always been my biggest fan. We are really close, and she always has my best interests in mind, regardless of the situation. When I was ten or eleven, I left my bike in a friend's front yard, and somebody stole it. Well, before too long I saw some kids with it down at the end of my block. I was small back then and really intimidated by the tough boys in the neighborhood. I stood outside our house, looking down the street at my bike, too scared to confront the boy who had it. Not Brittney. She was only five or six, a little girl with pigtails and beads in her hair. She grabbed my hand and said, "I'll go with you to get your bike back, Spank." She was so brave.

It didn't work. Those kids wouldn't give it back, and I returned home in tears. When Dad asked what I was crying about, I told him everything. His first move was to march down the street and snatch that bike up from those kids. His second move was to punish me for leaving it unattended in my friend's yard.

My little brother, Styles, is thirteen years younger than me and moved out with my mom when he was four or five. Until that point I took care of him like he was my own son, cutting his hair and driving him to preschool every day. I stopped being able to look after him like that once Mom left, but I never stopped loving him. I see a lot of my father in Styles; those two look exactly alike. I am proud of the man he's become.

The other family member I need to mention here is my father-in-law, Andrew Kennedy, who has been like a second father to me and has treated me like his own son. I am so lucky to have married into the Kennedy family.

The full list of people I'd like to thank is too extensive for this space, but I must name a few. There are those from my extended family: Carol Adams, Tony Adams, Tre Adams, Aaron Banks, Dedra Powell, Lamar Wright, and Toki Wright. There are those who made such a positive impact on me at the MPD: Kris Arneson, Tony Berryman, Jan Callaway, Troy Dillard, Rena Dudgeon, Tyler Edwards, Tim Hanks, Mike Johnson, Sohkum Klann, Art Knight, and Todd Kurth. There are the administrators at North High: Julie Anderson, Shawn Harris-Berry, Jeff Buzsta, and Kale Severson. There is my legion of coaches: Kriss Burrell, Abe Cass, Kyle Fox, Lance Horton, Willie Howard, Elijah Jackson, Kelley Jackson, Maurice Jones, Claude Labossiere, Tom Lachermeier, Tim Lawrence, Craig Merritt, Bo Powell, Chuck Simmons, Beulah Verdell, Marques Walker, Kevin Wiseman, Carrie Yeager, Cory Yeager, and the co-coaches who gave me my first shot at high school football, Ricky Williams and Tony Patterson. There are those within the Minnesota Twins family:

Rocco Baldelli, Jeff Beahen, Byron Buxton, Derek Falvey, Nick Gordon, Susan Bass Roberts, Dave St. Peter, Tommy Watkins, and the Pohlad Family. For those I didn't mention, please know that I appreciate you just as much as ever.

The process of writing this book was eye-opening for me. I realized how much anger and bitterness I'd pushed aside about my time as a cop, particularly when it came to my FTO training. It brought me back to times of helplessness, from being worried about how things might turn out if that trainer had prevented me from advancing, to the night of the riots, when I was thrown into the teeth of our community's outrage. Unpacking it all to tell this story brought a lot of things into focus.

Working with Jason helped me in ways I never expected. That he is not Black and did not share experiences similar to my own mattered less to me than talking with somebody who would tell this story in the best way possible. That he comes from someplace different than the Northside was actually a benefit. He asked questions that made me consider my own upbringing and how I came to the values I hold so dear—the kinds of things somebody more familiar with my situation might take for granted. It became an educational piece for both of us, and really helped bring my story to life.

In turn, I hope this book can bring positive change to those around me. That's already started. In January 2023, Showtime aired a four-part documentary about the North High football

program called *Boys in Blue*. Their original intent was to highlight a handful of coaches and players, including Deshaun Hill,
over the course of multiple seasons. When D-Hill was murdered, they pivoted, and the story—already one of perseverance
in the face of hardship—grew even more focused. My decision
to talk on camera about my disappointment with the University
of Minnesota's lack of interest in our program, in terms similar to those I express in this book, seemed to have an effect. A
couple of months later I received my first-ever visit from the
Golden Gophers' head coach, P. J. Fleck, along with several of
his assistants. P. J. told me that he recognized the excellence
at North High—that our kids get good grades and post high
test scores in addition to being really good football players—
and that he wanted to do a better job recruiting at our school. I
really appreciated that. The vast majority of our kids can't afford
to go to college unless it's paid for, and I've seen more than one
promising career end for lack of scholarship offers before it even
had a chance to start.

Here's hoping P. J. isn't the only one to notice.

—Charles Adams

The Northside of Minneapolis is not some Hollywood vision of
a poor, crime-riddled neighborhood. There are abundant single-
family homes with yards and fences, and tree-lined avenues that
provide a sense of suburban calm. I learned quickly how thin
that veneer runs when, touring the area with Charles one May

afternoon, we passed a streetside memorial marker for a recent victim of gun violence. Then another. And another. And another. I've been to many parts of many cities, and this place was unlike any I'd encountered. So was this story.

My job involves decoding people's lives, picking through them to find the relevant details and the parts that speak in recognizable terms about the human condition. This story—the first-person account of a Black man whose experience diverges from my own in so many essential ways—offered a particular challenge. As I considered whether to take on the project in the first place I could not stop wondering whether, as a white guy from Northern California, I even possessed enough reference points to sufficiently delve into a story like Charles's. Empathy, sure. Outrage? Of course. But this is more than a journalistic look at a subject, it's an autobiography. Knowing where somebody comes from—knowing it in your bones—allows for easy dissection of a given topic, because you already understand where to slice. For me, this story was not that.

Prior to finalizing the contract, I asked for a one-on-one meeting with Charles and laid my cards on the table. How do you feel, I asked, about a white man telling a Black man's story in which race plays such a prominent role? Charles didn't hesitate. "Man, you being here on this call and asking me that question tells me all I need to know," he said. And that was effectively that.

As our conversations progressed over the coming months, I pressed hard for details, not only about things that happened, but how Charles felt about it all. I tried to frame questions in ways that allowed space for Charles to unpack his perspective—sometimes so many ways that he chuckled in disbelief. "I thought I just answered that," he said on more than one occasion. Yeah, you did, but I needed to make sure the question was right, and covered every angle worth exploring. Charles's review of one of the early chapters included a note saying, "You perfectly captured how I feel." I could ask for no stronger endorsement, especially when it comes to a story as important as this one.

Traveling to Minneapolis to see the places we discussed was essential, especially the Northside neighborhood that is so integral to this story. We drove around in Charles's black SUV and he pointed out places of significance. He's unafraid in the Northside because people throughout the area recognize his car, decorated with a North High emblem on the tailgate, and give him due respect. Even Charles's rep wouldn't carry us through some blocks, however, for which I received a direct order: "Windows up. We don't take chances around here." Thanks, Charles, for your enduring availability and willingness to dive deep. Your desire for this story to be told is a key factor in whatever power this book holds.

Thanks also to everybody in Charles's Minneapolis circle who took time to speak with me, from coaches to police officers and beyond. Special thanks to Inspector Charlie Adams II, who hosted me in his Fourth Precinct office and subsequently spent many hours with me over multiple phone calls dissecting the complex idea of policing in Minneapolis.

Thanks also to our editor, Brant Rumble, with whose expert guidance I am by now familiar, as well as to Richard Abate at 3 Arts, and to my longtime and increasingly indispensable agent, Jud Laghi. And, of course, to my wife and kids, Laura, Mozi, and Reuben. The acknowledgment section of my first book, back in 2010, includes a story about me singing lullabies to our then-baby daughter from a ballpark telephone. When this book is published, that baby will have just left for college. Holy shit.

—Jason Turbow